T0149257

THE MIND AND PHILOSOPHY OF MAN IN HIS SEARCH FOR THE DIVINE

I. G. SOORMA

On the Prophet:

He did not report about anything except according to his inner vision and he did not order the following of his example except according to the truth of his conduct. He was in the presence of Allah, then he brought others to His Presence. He saw, then he related what he saw. He was sent forth as a guide, so he defined the limits of conduct.

- Al Hallaj, *The Tawasin*

Co-Authors:

Omar Soorma
Mark Dreisonstok

THE MIND AND PHILOSOPHY OF MAN
IN HIS SEARCH FOR THE DIVINE

Author Credits: Omar I. Soorma

iUniverse books may be ordered through booksellers or by contacting:

iUniverse
1663 Liberty Drive
Bloomington, IN 47403
www.iuniverse.com
1-800-Authors (1-800-288-4677)

ISBN: 978-1-5320-1623-3 (sc)
ISBN: 978-1-5320-1622-6 (e)

Library of Congress Control Number: 2017902848

Print information available on the last page.

iUniverse rev. date: 08/11/2017

Contents

Acknowledgement

This book, entitled *The Mind and Philosophy of Man in His Search for The Divine*, would not have been possible if my father, the late Ismail G. Soorma, had not spent writing about what interested him most during the last few years of his life.

My father's family hails from a small town of pre-independence India called Surat - Rander, south of Bombay, the financial capital of India. What was once a town is now a large, bustling city. After independence, my father and his extended family moved to Rangoon (now Yangon), Burma (today Myanmar), in southeast Asia. My father's immediate family consisted of my mother, my elder brother, my two sisters and myself. I lost my youngest sister in her early thirties to breast cancer. This was heart-breaking, as she was very dear to me.

Life was very good in the fertile land of Burma. It is a tropical country and rains a lot, but weather-wise, it is pleasant most of the time during the year, except during the very hot month of April. The people of Burma are very hospitable and friendly. Overall education standards were good. Burma's advantages once made it home to many non-ethnic Burmese. Indians, Chinese, and Europeans had settled down and called it home.

Unfortunately, the land of Burma has known political turmoil. The army took control of the government and replaced the then civilian cabinet of U Nu, Prime Minister of Burma, in the early 1950's. Education, business, economic and banking sectors were all nationalized.

Soon thereafter the standards of living and education declined. The pressures increased daily on all non-Burmese residents. Freedom of movement, print and speech were curtailed and restricted by the policies of the Revolutionary Council. In response to such pressure, the majority of foreign residents—Indians, Chinese and Europeans—left Burma to make their lives elsewhere.

My father's family was among those who were uprooted, as it were, overnight. Many of those displaced by events in Burma then resettled in Karachi, Pakistan. Others left for India, Europe, Australia and the USA. As my siblings and I grew up in different lands, my parents supported us every step of the way, both for our education and our daily needs. They always enjoined us to overcome any challenge or obstacle. They gave us the strength we needed to get through very hard times. My siblings and I appreciate deeply everything our parents have done for us in life.

Some of my parents' extended family in Karachi were very helpful, including Dawood Jamal and family as well as Bilal and Tin Lay Raschid's family, who were very kind and the most generous family friends one could ever wish for in the world during our times of need. Without their assistance, our experience in a new country would have been far more difficult. I wish especially to thank my Uncle Dawood, for extending his help in the hour of need during our years of resettling.

This is the first book I have co-authored. It has been a great experience, though difficult at times. My sincere and deep thanks are extended to Dr. Mark Dreisonstok, PhD (Georgetown University), Professor of English, highly knowledgeable in philosophy, theology, and literature, who served as chief editor of this book. He is an expert in several fields yet at the same time a very patient and humble person. Without his help, this project would not have got off the ground. His wife Winnie Dreisonstok, MA (St. John's College, Annapolis), helped in translations and research. His father Erwin and daughter Cordelia also were also very helpful in this project. Dr. John M. Bozeman, PhD (Virginia Tech), an expert in religious studies, was of great assistance in locating and advising on obscure citations in the field of theology. Thanks to all of them!

My father, a lawyer by profession, a graduate of what was once the Law College of the University of Rangoon, was in his own right a philosopher and scholar. An avid collector of books, both Eastern and Western, he was very knowledgeable and a voracious reader in the fields of philosophy and religion. He was by nature a teacher: sincere, humble and a very private person of calm demeanor. He began writing this book in Rangoon and continued in Karachi. In his last few years, his health declined, and he lost focus due to multiple health issues.

I continued with the project a year after his passing while I was studying and doing graduate work at the University of Akron, Ohio, USA. It was not at all easy, being in the scientific fields of biology, biochemistry, medical technology, management and infection control.

I spent some years reading extensively and researching the worlds of philosophy, theology, comparative religion and poetry - Eastern and Western (Victorian especially) as well as Middle Eastern. Gaining an appreciation of the Scriptures of the Holy Qur'an, the Holy Bible, and other well-documented, recognized scriptures as well as the classics of the ancient world was crucial for this project.

There are many to thank for their vital and generous contributions towards this book. My heart goes out to all loved ones in my family. Special thanks to my loving and beautiful wife Salma, who has always stood with me for her help and understanding during my busy days. A deep appreciation and debt are owed to my two sisters, Hajra and Zulekha, for their important input towards this book. Deep thanks to my late uncle from my father's side, Dr. Azam Soorma and his wife for their love, kindness, encouragement and support.

This project would not have been possible without the help from Kelly Ness, a good friend from MedStar D.C. Hospital, for typing this manuscript (partly hand-written, partly typed on a vintage manual typewriter) to a computerized format.

I am also thankful to Imam Yunus of Springfield, Ohio, for his help with the verses and chapters of the Holy Qur'an as well as to my friend Omar Mohammed for pointing out and correcting the quotes from the Holy Qur'an. My thanks are extended to my son Muzammil for helping me out with the computer work as well as providing support and encouragement. A final word of thanks go out to Kate Van Zant, Mars Alma and the author-friendly iUniverse Penguin Book publishing house team in Indiana, USA.

Omar I. Soorma
Lewis Center, Ohio, January 2017.

REMEMBRANCE OF
ISMAIL G. SOORMA

"In the delicate clatter of trays and saucers, in the soft rustle of feminine hospitality, in the common catechism about cream and sugar," it is written in the *Book of Tea*, "is the art of concealing beauty that you may discover it, of suggesting what you dare not reveal. It is the noble secret of laughing at yourself, calmly yet thoroughly, and is thus humor itself,—the smile of philosophy." The serving of tea to which the gifted Japanese essayist Okakura Kakuzō refers is indeed culturally very unique, for it is not only about the consumption of tea but the beautiful elegance with which it is served, for example, in tea cups of chinaware with tea covers along with them and the atmosphere which it creates is suitable to discussions on weighty matters.

Lahpet, or the special tea in Burma where I spent my childhood, is served with different traditional accompaniments. Tea is dry-roasted before boiling water is mixed with it in order to make it green. It is served plain or sweetened by using cream or milk, and in Burma, now Myanmar, it is sometimes prepared with either black or sweet dry tea and made in the Indian way, which is sweetened and brewed with condensed milk. Tea serving at our home played a very strong role in our life in Burma in developing friendships, building cultural bridges and engaging in deep discussions about life.

I recall as a child serving tea to visitors and close friends of my father as hospitality and respect paid to them during visits or during discussions they were having on metaphysical subjects such as theology and philosophy – conversations which to me as a teenager then were utterly incomprehensible. I remember as well the elegance and graciousness shown by my mother, a lady of enormous kindness and a devoted wife and mother who always extended her respect and friendship towards Dad's friends, companions, and colleagues, following a custom to serve traditional green or Indian tea, one unique to or rather adapted by Burma.

It has remained imprinted on my mind to extend respect and accommodate for differences of cultures as an attitude to be learned, emulated and translated into life. I owe who I am as a human being who endeavors to be gentle, humble, sincere, decent and honest in dealings with my fellow beings and accept weaknesses and frailties in myself and others to this tradition around the serving of tea on such special social occasions, one of the many gifts my father gave to me. You could say that another of his gifts was this book (written privately and never published until now), in which he wrote down many of his ideas and speculations about life and which give me an idea of the content of the exalted philosophical discussions which took place over tea servings between my father and his friends during those special days of my childhood in mid-twentieth-century Burma.

Ismail G. Soorma, my father, was always imaginative and philosophical about life. He was by profession a lawyer, though he never practiced law. He was instead a businessman, and perhaps part of his success stemmed from his honest, straightforward nature and appearance:

he was fair and handsome, with curly hair and a finely chiseled nose. Although trained in law and active in business, at heart he was a scholar and a philosopher with an intuitive and inquiring mind and a wonderful ability to listen and to absorb. He was always an avid collector of books: his remarkable collection of books on philosophy, history, literature and the arts would be any researcher's dream. His collection of paintings and artworks was equally breathtaking, and to be found in our home were reproductions of famous artworks like *The Last Supper* and *Mona Lisa* of Leonardo DaVinci, which he had framed on display in his drawing room. He would remember the names of all his books. I remember once borrowing Tolstoy's *War and Peace* and *Anna Karenina* to read and he would remind me to return them. On birthdays and festive occasions, he would give us books as gifts. We would read voraciously and wait for more.

Among my father's favorite writers were Shakespeare, Goethe, Sir Muhammad Iqbal, Rumi and DaVinci. He was a loner and would rarely socialize, but he was very benevolent towards his family, friends and employees. He had some good friends in Rangoon, Burma. One such family friend was U Raschid, who was the former Minister of Industry, Mines and Labour in the first elected Prime Minister U Nu's cabinet, the first elected Chairman of the International Labour Organisation (1961) and a political ally of General Aung San, the father of Burma. He would also discuss philosophy and politics with U Raschid's two sons: Bilal (an accomplished architect) and Salman (a psychiatrist and philosopher), now living in the United States and the United Kingdom respectively.

My father was a teacher in his student days and was thus very particular about diction and pronunciation. One word uttered by any of us children, and he would go into detail. His enormous, unabridged Webster dictionary would be referred to our attention. He would make sure we absorbed the details and that our phonetics and syllables were correct. Ever an idealist, my father loved nature and beauty. His aesthetic sense would often make him grouchy about many things not suiting his nature. He would go into quiet meditations. In this same spirit, he would be fond of good cuisine. He expected perfect meals. My mother, a very kind lady, would always take good care of my father and was an excellent cook who prepared meals to perfection.

He would go for long walks in the wilderness alone or with his children. He seldom went to the movies and was not particular about clothes either. I remember my mother often got piqued about this. Yet he was particular about hygiene and cleanliness. He disliked uncouth behavior and therefore placed stress on politeness and self-respect.

My father loved to listen to classical music, and his favorites were Mozart, Beethoven and Chopin. His collections of Urdu publications on Iqbal were the envy of researchers on Iqbal, and included studies of Iqbal and Goethe and in particular a comparison, perhaps in the cross-cultural spirit of this present book, of Iqbal's "Shikwa" to Goethe's *Faust*—of the German poet who admired "The nightingale [...] The spring attracted her again—She [...] Sings the old dear refrain" and the Indian poet who wished "hearts open up with the song of this lonely nightingale" ("Shikwa"). Perhaps my father was attracted to these works because he marveled at the beauty of nature and God's omnipotence. He always wrote along philosophical lines, ever stressing the strength of man's relationship to Nature and God.

In my father's final years, he wrote this book; then he lost all interest in worldly affairs and departed. He was always concerned about the moral disintegration of man and society. We love and miss him. He was a special dad, a unique and solitary person who would have understood the American poet Poe when he wrote in his poem "Alone:"

> From childhood's hour I have not been
> As others were—I have not seen
> As others saw—I could not bring
> My passions from a common spring.

My father also lived in his own world and could not reconcile himself with the vagaries of human nature and dishonesty of people in general.

It is sad that he did not live to see his great grandchildren, as he would have been delighted to play with them. I am sure he must be happy where he is, enjoying himself in the eternal bliss of the afterlife. In the meantime, the reader of this book is invited to explore each individual writer's original contributions to better Man's condition on earth through his lofty philosophies and religious beliefs, as my father does in the following book and did, indeed, throughout his life.

Omar I. Soorma
Lewis Center, Ohio, January 2017.

Preface

William Shakespeare's works are among the great books of the world, not merely because of their beauty of language, but also because they examine ideas and themes that have fascinated readers and provoked discussion for centuries. Mention of his comedic play *Love's Labour's Lost* is *apropos* here, for it is Shakespeare's brilliant commentary on how reading and learning are doomed when not connected to life itself.

In the play, Shakespeare addresses the importance of education as King Ferdinand of Navarre and three courtiers attempt to create an intellectual feast upon which "the mind shall banquet" (Act I, scene i, line 25) by studying the great books of Western civilization. "Our court shall be a little academe" (Act I, scene i, line 13), King Ferdinand announces, as he turns his palace into an academy of learning filled with books. While the king's intentions may be noble, the vows under which he and his fellow scholars undertake their quest are less so:

1.) They must devote themselves exclusively to study for a period of three years;
2.) They must sleep only three hours per night;
3.) They must fast (only one meal per day, and on one day there will be a total fast); and
4.) There must be no contact with women or the outside world during this time. Women are similarly banished from the court of Navarre itself.

Unfortunately, the King himself is soon forced to break his own pledge as the Princess of France arrives on a state visit, attended by three ladies of the French Court. As might be surmised, the king and his three fellow scholars are forced to attend to the princess and her three ladies at the expense of their reading and studies. In the course of their hosting duties, the king and his men come to realize the sterility of education found solely through isolated contemplation of books; as one of the main characters, Lord Berowne, states in Act IV:

> From women's eyes this doctrine I derive:
> They sparkle still the right Promethean fire;
> They are the books, the arts, the academes,
> That show, contain and nourish all the world... (Scene iii, lines 347-50)

Shakespeare is not simply claiming that there is wisdom to be found in feminine beauty. Rather, he is saying engagement with the world is utterly essential; without it, philosophical and literary works have but static value. We should, in fact, be wary of "an education which (merely) quickens the Intellect, and leaves the heart hollower and harder than before." (Albert Pike, *Morals and Dogma*, Chapter 2)

The book before you, composed by the late Ismail G. Soorma, Esq., embodies the essence of Shakespeare's insight. Throughout the work, the author references great masterpieces of philosophy, religion, nature, art and psychology, distilling the eternal truths found within each. At the same time, these great books and ideas exist in dialogue with each other, creating between them a lively discussion that stimulates the reader to come to his own understanding of the universe in which he lives. This invigorating elixir is particularly welcome today in our technological age in which intense, prolonged reading has become less a crucial element in the formation of one's understanding of the world and where specialization has supplanted broad general education and reflection. This book is a work of scholarship, but in this important sense which has become almost lost to scholars of our time.

In having the privilege and pleasure to edit this manuscript, I was reminded of other works also written during the first half to the mid-point of the twentieth century: *The Importance of Living* by Lin Yutang, *A Mencken Chrestomathy* by H.L. Mencken, and *How to Read a Book* by Mortimer Adler. Each of these works, though quite different both from one another and from the present study, embodies two common characteristics: the author's encyclopedic understanding of the finest literature of his and earlier eras, and his ability to synthesize reading and experience into a compelling new worldview. The reader of each work is thus engaged, enriched and informed simultaneously.

During the course of editing, I have repeatedly been struck by the fact that even though the author of the present book and I never met, we were each educated through our encounters with multiple cultures and religious traditions. The particular cultures that we experienced differ, I found remarkable affinities and commonalities in our ethical understandings. Further, each of us values broad education, the embrace of challenging ideas and notions, and a refusal to see barriers between such supposedly different disciplines as literature and philosophy, psychology and religion. Throughout my editing, I have therefore emphasized this book's universal appeal, reediting the order of certain sections and paragraphs to enhance the flow ideas, and, in some cases, clarifying now-obscure phrasing. On the other hand, I have preserved as much as possible the vocabulary and stylistic choices of the author so that the reader may fully appreciate the unique flavor of the author's style. An index I have created at the end of the book serves as a reference to which primary texts are discussed in each section. More than that, it serves as a list of books for reading, reflection, and discussion—in many cases, expanding the traditional European and East Asian canon with the inclusion of mystical and Islamic/Sufist works.

I met Mr. Omar Soorma in the spring of 2013. Although he is a scientist active in the field of biochemistry and attained an M.S. Degree on full scholarship in biology at the University of Akron, Ohio, I found him to be a man of wide-ranging academic, philosophical and aesthetic interests. He is also very much as he describes his father in the poignant remembrance which precedes this preface: a private man of humble personality dedicated to his wife, son and siblings. Mr. Soorma has contributed in immeasurable ways to the editing of this manuscript, and I appreciate especially his being so open to my suggestions and giving me such latitude to edit, reconstruct and—in some cases—augment with new paragraphs and references the original manuscript. I would like to acknowledge his help with achieving a better understanding of Sufism and writers in the Islamic tradition.

The universalistic approach contained in this book may not be error-free, and it is not the final word on the great ideas discussed within it. Rather, it is an invitation to the reader to explore further these ideas on his own, an invitation enhanced by the concluding index compiled in the form of a list of the Great Books referenced throughout – for as Nietzsche writes in *The Gay Science,*

> Es lockt dich meine Art und Sprach',
> Du folgest mir, du gehst mir nach?
> Geh nur dir selber treulich nach: —
> So folgst du mir – gemach! gemach!
>
> Attracted by my style and talk
> You'd follow, in my footsteps walk?
> Follow yourself unswervingly.
> So — careful! — shall you follow me.
>   (Paul V. Cohn and Maude D. Petre, trans.)

Dr. Mark Dreisonstok, M.A. (Universität Freiburg im Breisgau), Ph.D. (Georgetown University) Washington, D.C., February 2015.

CHAPTER 1

The World of Appearances

" . . . a lotus-flower rising out of clouds." -
Lafcadio Hearn

Man knows appearances and studies only appearances.
Baltasar Gracián, a Jesuit writer of the Spanish Baroque,
observed: "Things pass for what they seem, not for what
they are. Few see inside, many take to the outside." ("Reality
and Appearance," *Hand Oracle and the Art of Prudence*).
Even as realist and worldly a philosopher as Machiavelli
observed that "men in general make judgments more by
appearances than by reality." (*The Prince*) As a creature
of the senses, man is in bondage to things and objects in
the external world. Everything outside him profoundly
affects him. There is no center in him to hold the tumult
and clamor of his sense-impressions and desires.

His senses respond only to a fragment of the world,
and his view of it is colored by them. Whatever it really
is, he sees it in a certain way. It is not that the senses show
him an illusory world, as the Hindus believe. They call the
world maya and in this sense proclaim that "Hard it is / To
pierce that veil divine of various shows (*maya* or illusion),"
as we read in the classic Hindu scripture Bhagavad Gita
(7: 25; Sir Edwin Arnold, trans). The same viewpoint
carried over into Buddhism: "Buddha, like Kapila [a
Hindu sage depicted in the Bhagavad Gita], maintained

that this world had no absolute reality, that it was a snare and an illusion," writes Friedrich Max Müller, scholar of comparative religion. Buddhist scriptures such as the Lankavatara Sutra, with its image that the world is like a mirage of water, expand this view further. The Hindu and Buddhist view that objective Reality is an illusion runs contrary to Islamic belief. It is closer to the truth to say that man is merely shown a fringe of Reality; even then, he seldom penetrates beyond the surface of things. This is due to man's limited insight, however, not because the world itself is all an illusion.

Man's mode of perceiving objects is conditioned by his constitution and may not be shared by other "beings." There are invisible realities surrounding his sense-world on all sides.

The senses appear to show us everything on the same scale, though they are of varying size and shapes and at various distances. The eye can pass without any difficulty from a star to a cell for analysis under a microscope. Yet we are passing from one order of things to quite a different order. How can this all be taken on the same scale?

Our world, the world of experience, has a reality which is only relative. What we perceive through the senses is *not* the "thing as it is" but just a relative aspect of the "thing as it is."

We cannot know or understand the Universe merely through the method of science. All of our explanations are really descriptions of "processes," which in themselves continue to tantalize us as an enigma.

Man is not changed internally by discoveries of phenomena. Once the novelty of each wears off, he expects more. The quality of his consciousness undergoes no change. He remains far from the abiding sense of the awe and wonder that they should infuse in him. The most sublime experience for man would be to experience this sense of awe and wonder.

The Universe man knows is only one aspect of the total spectrum of Reality. Our space and time are particular conditions under which we humans have to pass our existence.

Man explores the Universe but is hardly aware that he will not be able to fathom it beyond a certain limit, for his own nature sets this condition on him. His habit is to think "outwards;" he is preoccupied with overcoming the outward problems and challenges that stubbornly confront him.

Knowledge tells us more about the knower than about that which is known, for man's nature is deeply implicated in the process and colors everything he knows or does. The observer cannot be separated from that which is observed.

All that is most real to man lies in his interior life, *his life within*. Yet he is ever a victim of self-deceptions and illusions. Every man born into the world is actually a new starting point. He is not only in the world, for a world is in him, a universe in its multifaceted dimensions. The visible Universe, stretching out infinitely before man, is a wondrous scheme on different planes and dimensions of a scale that baffles the mind, and man, as a very complex creature in it, has within him a scale immeasurable and of different levels of mind, consciousness and understanding.

Intuition and mystic vision alone can penetrate the fathomless depths.

If man flaunts an inferior explanation of Reality, it will "backfire" on him. He will shrink, become stunted in his interior life, and thus estrange himself from the potentialities of his being which lie within his inner self. Hermann Hesse provides us with a far more edifying vision—that of

> One who has found the path to the inner self,
> One who has, in glowing self-meditation,
> Sensed the inner wisdom
> That his senses choose to view God and the world
> As image and parable –
> To such a one as this every action and thought
> Become a dialogue with one's own soul
> Wherein are contained God and the world.
>
> ("Der Weg nach Innen;" Mark Dreisonstok, trans.)

A materialistic outlook is not only superficial but limits us psychologically. We become incapable of reaching higher levels of conscious experience if we persist in relying purely on the "evidence of things seen," to turn around the phrase of St. Paul, who wrote of "the substance of things hoped for, the evidence of things *not* seen." (Hebrews 11: 1)

Chapter 2

Man Is Not a Unity

There was the Door to which I found
no Key;
There was the Veil through which I might
not see...
(Omar Khayyam, *Rubáiyát,* XXXII;
Edward FitzGerald, trans.)

Every man believes he possesses individuality, full consciousness and will, yet this is not true. As a man is in the world of appearances, covered by veils of self-deceptions and illusions, he is neither an individual in the true meaning of the word even conscious, properly speaking. His life passes by in a state of unreality. He lives, as it were, in darkness.

The German writer Heinrich Heine depicted in several of his verses the still, silent and beautiful Lotus in the moonlight along the Ganges River in India, but this Lotus is not merely a picturesque image or a flower symbolic only of the longing of European Romantic poets. It has a special meaning in Hinduism and Buddhism, for the Lotus has its roots in the loathsome mud and grows in dark swampy water. Yet it emerges above the water to form a flower of intense beauty. Similarly, human beings live in the world of suffering and must transcend this sad state of affairs to something ever higher, to something more sublime – to Nirvana, to "Paradise [to be] ever refreshed by the dew of the same Lotus." (Lady Murasaki Shikibu, *The Tale of Genji*; Arthur Waley, trans.) The Lotus is a symbol in nature of the "great mystery [of] life rising out of death," as Albert Pike states in *Morals and Dogma* (Chapter 25). For the present book, perhaps we can think of the Lotus as man's attempt to break free from the muddy waters of materialism and ascend upwards, Lotus-like, into the higher realms of spirituality and the intellect.

Tragically, this vital fact is hidden even from persons of high intelligence. Western psychology itself has generally overlooked this most vital knowledge.

Man, it is surprising to learn, does not possess will. He consists merely of a web of self-wills – self-wills which are always in conflict with one another and forever tugging and pulling him in contrary directions.

A man is ever-changing and thus never one and the same for long. He is a kaleidoscope of a thousand "I's." and every stimulus changes the pattern of his moods. These moods govern him: his feeling of "I" is subservient to his mood, and every "I" produces its own state. Yet man thinks he knows and understands himself, and there is truly no greater illusion than this.

Practically all of man's inner states are different forms of illusion and self-deception. He takes the "state" of the moment as his true self.

Plutarch, the Greek historian of antiquity, remarked: "...each one of us is made up of ten thousand different and successive states, a scrap-heap of units, a mob of individuals." (A.O. Prickard, trans.) In his novel *Steppenwolf,* the German writer Hermann Hesse notes in an unusual but effective metaphor that "man is an onion made up of a hundred different peels" – as it were, a fabric of varied "threads."

The French philosopher Henri Bergson affirmed in *Creative Evolution*:

> "I pass from state to state. I am warm or cold. I am merry or sad. I work or do nothing. I look at what is around me or I think of something else. Sensations, Feelings, Volitions, Ideas - such are the changes, into which my existence is divided and which color it in turns. I change, then, without ceasing."

Sir Muhammad Iqbal, the great Indian poet-philosopher, observed: "...there is nothing static in my inner life; all is a constant mobility, an unceasing flux of states, a perpetual flow in which there is no halt or resting place." (*The Reconstruction of Religious Thought in Islam*)

The psychological teaching of William Blake, the great English visionary and mystic poet, showed man as nothing but his states passing between Innocence and Experience. If man were nothing but his states and identified himself with them, how would he attain self-hood, or unity of being?

Attend to the word "identify" and realize the depth of meaning it conveys!

As long as man has the illusion that he is a "unity," he cannot change within himself. He is turned only "outwards" and believes in appearances. He exists in a world that he does not really understand.

There are a thousand things which prevent a man from awakening, things which keep him in the power of his phantasies and self-delusions. Whatever thoughts, feelings and imagination with which a man identifies himself would profoundly change things for him.

No man can change himself, without altering the feeling of himself. This is immensely difficult. We do not realize that in order to change anything in ourselves, everything else must change in us, lest—by trying to change one thing—we may bring about unintended consequences and ultimately wrong results in other areas. Change of being is not haphazard patch-work, for the entire way of life has to change.

As we exist currently, we have no real sense of "I," for the real "I" would require a new state of the individual, an entirely fresh quality of consciousness. We have to plunge to a deeper level of reality within. Conceit or self-idolatry, in fact any feeling that panders to egoism, merely creates the illusion of a stable "I," whereas the full potentiality of "I" as is now extremely remote from us.

Our ordinary feeling of "I" could never lead us to understand things rightly, that is, to know the proper order of things. Reality can only be known when there is a transformation of the feeling of "I" in us.

Higher levels of conscious experience are latent in man. In the highest flight of intuition and mystic vision, evil no longer appears as evil because the true and necessary relation of all things is then apprehended in the right way.

If we could grasp in a moment of intuitive understanding the totality of things apart from the senses, we would come to perceive the Universe as a unity in its awesome wholeness, as "all are but parts of one stupendous whole." (Alexander Pope, *An Essay on Man*, Epistle X)

There is a proverb in the literature of Sufi, the Ascetic and Mystical system of Islam: "If the senses were eliminated, the world would appear as a unity."

The reason is our senses continually deceive us and lead us astray.

We take ourselves for granted and never *see* (how significant *that word* is!) what we actually are. Though no one is really satisfied with his lot in life, one does not *realize* that his level of being attracts the kind of life he leads. What meaning is hidden here, and it takes an extraordinary and creative effort to fathom it!

Man passes the days of his life in a somnambulistic state – unfeeling and insensitive to the meaning of things. He is a creature of habit, dead to himself and dead to the nature of things. He will never realize what he actually is unless he earnestly studies all of his habits and flaws and makes a ceaseless effort to overcome those which impede and block his self-evolution. He nonetheless spends his time and energy in negative emotions, in phantasies, in small talk and gossip. How can he then develop beyond what he is, a mechanical man?

The lack of unity in man is the real source of his troubles and weaknesses. His inner life is in constant discord, and he is divided against his own self. He never really *is*! Reflect a moment so that the meaning sink into consciousness.

Behind almost everyone there stretch years of an empty and meaningless life, wasted in indulgence of desires, in ignorance and pretense, carried along the stream of conventions. There is no real direction—only a drifting, aimless deception of one's self and the deception of others, with self-justification at every bend and the avoidance of unpleasant facts about one's own self. This life oozes with lies.

No one dares to face oneself and one's real position. Only an extreme situation, a very violent shock, can shake one up to the core of his being and enable one to pass from the drift and confusion, from the lies of his false life to the meanings the terrible impact of harsh reality could alone register.

The meaning of every single thing can change. If it changes, our relationship to it, too, will change.

Awareness in most of us is confined to an extremely narrow sphere, with all its petty interests and futilities. We have no proper consciousness of one another. Trivial matters occupy all of our time, and we are little more than creatures of the moment. Anything spoken about a higher life carries no meaning for us in our state. To live a more conscious life, one has to be able to distinguish between inner states and outer events and then engage them, after observing their nature, with the right inner state. By a man's state is meant how he accepts an event.

A man's capacity of life depends on his inner condition, on the quality of his inner states. It is a crime against man's own self if he is unmindful of the state of this interior world, invisible and inaccessible to others, however close they may be to him.

Man can exist "asleep" or he can live "awake." The consequences of this are far-reaching. In a state of "sleep," he leaves no trace or mark behind, tantamount to a confession of failure that his life was devoid of meaning and purpose. The awakened one evolves and fulfills the human meaning of his life. As Ayn Rand reminds us in *Anthem,* however, "The secrets of this earth are not for all men to see, but only for those who will seek them."

Life is really a series of events, happening at different levels and clustering around the axis of the day. These events draw people and things into various relations at different moments, move them about, and then pass away. A single event could be stretched to fill up all one's time and leave nothing for other matters. It is not the events of the day such as someone has been rude and disagreeable, or some matter has gone wrong that should be of prime concern to us, but how we have reacted to them all. Our real life dwells in our inner states, and if they are positive, no event need overwhelm us with fear and anxiety. We must learn to remain passive to some events, not to react to them at all. We can do this provided we are "awake" within.

Albert Pike takes up this point in *Morals and Dogma*, reminding us that the purpose of all great literature, philosophy and orations is to awaken those who are asleep:

> There are many things in us of which we are not distinctly conscious. To waken that slumbering consciousness into life, and so to lead the soul up to the Light, is one office of every great ministration to human nature, whether its vehicle be the pen, the pencil, or the tongue. (Chapter 12)

To learn to be passive or stoic to a situation is wisdom, yet it takes much time to see what this means. This attitude is not one of indifference, for it is useless just to keep an indifferent posture, for we are then false in our behavior. A mollusk can teach us how to take an event, either expanding into it or to drawing away from it.

How marvelous it is when we shake ourselves free from our habitual way of regarding life. With insight into ourselves, we can meet events in a conscious way. First, however, we must rid ourselves of conceit and complacency alike. This will be far from easy, for we have to observe our inner and outer behavior and take mental photographs of our behavior over the years. Inevitably, they will shatter our vanity, but for a long time we shall still swing between the old state and the new.

Consider how damaging our inner life can become. Negative states attract other negative states to themselves, and we pivot on recurring states. All the unpleasant and disagreeable things keep rushing into our mind, while the pleasant things just get blotted out in a flash. We observe this around us daily as a grey atmosphere covers the affairs of life, and the pall refuses to lift.

Contrary to a very common belief, to change life *is not* to change outer circumstances. It is to change *our* reactions. Life *is not* action, as we all believe, but reaction to impressions and events that we continually receive from outer life. We have to make ourselves passive (how difficult that is) *to our own reactions*, not to those to whom we are reacting. There really is no freedom in merely reacting, which is being mechanical.

A sublime form of action is non-action, the ability to refrain from reacting to urges and impulses that possess us. This is a very active and dynamic from of self-discipline. It is one of the hardest things in the world to control our reactions to impressions, situations and happenings life throws our way. How many can take hold, of themselves, and check their thoughts, feelings, desires, impulses and speech? To have acquired that self-discipline is to have reached a level of balanced perspective, making one superbly competent at any task to be undertaken. We must come to this understanding that "impressions" can be transformed. The senses now have such a powerful mesmeric effect on us that we find it difficult to understand how this can even be. The result of transformation would be the sublime form of action: *non-action*, which must be implemented as a *conscious* response to all events. Could one be more creative?

How tragic it is that after a certain age, most of us experience, as a rule, no new impressions. We become jaded. Now impressions are always fresh and new at every moment, but as a result of the deadness of our vision, they merely bring up the same old associations, making our life grey and empty. For if a person is enmeshed in material things instead of detached from them, life begins to pall, and a creeping feeling of unreality steals over him, more so as he passes into old age. How right was the British Romantic poet William Wordsworth that such freshness of experience is left behind in childhood, to our detriment: "At length the Man perceives it to die away, and fade into the light of common day." ("Ode to Intimations of Immortality from Recollections of Early Childhood")

It is imperative, then, to select and arrange our daily impressions and respond meaningfully to them alone, in order to develop and evolve as people.

He who seeks insight into himself does not follow life's direction but rather follows his own direction in life. There is a world of difference between the two meanings, for everything that happens in life *is a means*, not an end. Yet people take material life as an end itself, and they do things with this in mind, obsessively seeking results. If things do not turn out as wished, desired and expected, they feel disappointed and miserable.

We have to work against the adverse circumstances in which we find ourselves. Life is not an unmixed blessing. Born rich or poor, powerful or meek and helpless, all of us have our own particular—and in a certain sense unique— problems and difficulties, which, no matter how we feel about them, have to be confronted and cannot be wished away. Life never runs as we would wish it to run or expect it to go. Layer after layer of pride and vanity, conceit and ignorance have to be passed before we can perceive convincingly for ourselves that we have weaknesses and flaws of character.

What an arduous and long process that is!

It is indeed strange to become conscious of oneself and stranger still to become conscious of another person's actual, objective existence.

A man is glued to his senses, active and alive in those parts of his which are turned outwards. His real and essential self lies behind this external sense-based side. It is this inner self that has to be developed through self-observation and conscious effort. This self-observation is an objective effort, not the unhealthy subjective interest we take in ourselves. Writes the German mystical poet Novalis: "The seat of the soul is that point at which the inner world and the outer world come into contact." (Mark Dreisonstok, trans.)

The man at the mercy of the senses is the man who has no inner life, for whom everything lies in the outside world. Bright though this world seems, he actually lives in darkness, ignorant of the real nature of things.

The interior world of man, which is made up of psychological states, is a vast place, and one has to know it lies not only in the exterior world. Bright though this world is, he actually lives in darkness, ignorant of the real nature of things.

The interior world of man, which is made up of psychological states, is a vast place, and one has to know not only *who* lives within it but also *where* it is lived.

An ordinary man behaves internally just as he pleases. He may be civil and polite on the surface, yet his inner self may be like the hiss of a snake. It never occurs to him that it matters profoundly how he thinks and feels about others.

The ideas a man learns from life are confused and of baffling contradictions, and there is an incredible lack of unity and meaning in the life he lives from day to day as he passes time. Its cares and stresses fatigue him, and everyone is enmeshed in this regard in one way or another. A man's situation begins to change only when he realizes that he alone has to bear the burden of his life and work without pause or rest so that he can become capable of resisting the particular mechanical effects on his inner and outer self. Could any work be more difficult?

CHAPTER 3

Human Destiny

"Of what thing did he create him (man)?
Of a small life-germ He created him, then,
He made him according to a measure."
- Holy Qur'an (80-18, 19)

Man's life is a book of perennially teasing study. It has had a beginning, and the last word will never come to be written.

There is the role of chance, for he does not choose the parents to whom he will be born or the place where he will be born. This itself is of such a profound import to his existence that its traces will never be erased on his being as long as he lives. People imagine that being born in a privileged house bestows on the child a favorable destiny and being born in a hovel condemns the child to perpetual hardship and misery. That may be generally true in a superficial sense, but there are twists and turns of life: through life's quirks and oddities, the child of the hovel may end up with respect, prestige and honors and the child of the privileged house hanged on the gallows. This is where Destiny takes charge with its implacable laws. Its other name is Character, for in a profound sense, destiny and character are two sides of the same fateful coin.

Human destiny is not pre-determined but self-determined. Destiny is God's decree concerning the nature of things. It is conditioned by His knowledge of their essential nature. Whatever destiny decrees is actually decreed by the thing itself. God's foreknowledge does not preclude man's freedom of choice, and the Divine Decree does not take away freedom of choice from man. God has decreed man to choose to act or not to act as his inclination leads him.

Just as there is no event unrelated to Divine Knowledge, so is there no event unrelated to Divine Will. The Will of God is related to all acts of man in their actualization according to his own choice. The relationship between Divine Will and human choice, far from negating man's freedom of choice, actually confirms and seals it.

Our perception and understanding shape our will. Destiny, understanding, and freedom of choice have an organic relationship. It is our power of understanding that sets the will in motion. The will makes a choice and proceeds to act on it. The more real or authentic our thoughts and feelings are, the more conscious is our will, and hence our acts. We are enabled to see the consequences of our acts with keener insight and escape the traps of an impulsive choice. Our knowledge and understanding are equal to our responsibility. We are forgiven our ignorance if we are not really aware of our words and our acts. When we are conscious, *fully alive to the consequences of our choice*, we must pay the price of our misdeeds. We stand exposed, and if we still persist in our evil ways, destiny visits upon us dire results.

Impulse is the very antithesis of a conscious act. It is wayward and willful, for when impulse is in the driver's seat, man is a mere slave under its baneful influence. When man has freed himself from the blind, subjective control of his impulses, he reaches objective understanding. He emerges into light from a dark tunnel, and his sight is keen and clear.

There is no end to things which attract or repel man, and when he is driven by impulse, he is changed into the very essence of those things which obsess him. His Destiny is "weigh[ed] with equal hand" and measured in all its nuances. (Homer, *Iliad*, Book XXII; Alexander Pope, trans.) Nothing is missed, and everything is taken into account.

Man swings back and forth between rest and activity. Rest, though, is a relative state, while contention and struggle are the very atmosphere in which he breathes and lives. Tension is the creation of contention and struggle, and without tension, man cannot live. Yet the wrong sort of tension digs a man's grave, and the right kind of tension is the right atmosphere in which he can evolve. Today this notion might go under the terms "good stress" and "bad stress," but this verity was observed long ago. This is the "trial of man" of the Qur'anic meaning—man passing from state to state:

> Oh, I swear by the afterglow of sunset,
> And by the night and all that it enshrouded,
> And by the moon when she is at the full,
> that, ye shall journey on, from plane to plane.
> - Holy Qur'an (84 16-19)

Strangely, as man evolves, his life takes on the character of a higher determinism, a paradox touching his existence at many points. The more it comes under a "higher determinism," the freer it becomes. Under the higher law, God himself directs it.

The strictest determinist goes about his life as if he possessed the freedom of will he has denied others. What would be the point of asking man to mend his ways if we maintained at the same time that he were bound and trussed? Man is both free and determined—in himself, free and creative, and yet determined by the presence of certain elements over which he had no control. These are situations which are unalterable and which he is powerless to control.

Freedom of choice is freedom of action, for action in itself implies "choice." Once a choice is made, it becomes irreversible. In acting in any situation in a given manner, a man unconsciously determines his own future. The future, however, is not given as of itself. It actually unfolds in action, for all action is directed into the future. Therefore, to say that the future is already determined is to assert there is no "future." By its inherent nature, the "future" is indeterminate. A determinate "future" is paradoxically a "future" that is already "past" – and passed.

Man can never escape from the dilemma of making a "choice." Alternatives and options press upon him from all sides. Once, however, he "chooses," he invariably sets a limit to his freedom of action and inevitably binds himself to all the consequences of his "choice." Yet man is never alone or completely isolated, as he is part and parcel of the world, pressing upon him from all sides. Therefore, his choices are never made in a void. Other factors, beyond his power and control, hedge and restrict his freedom of action.

It bears repetition that man's inner states continually modify his destiny. Everyone creates, in this sense, his own destiny, according to his level of his being and understanding. As is his heart, so is his life. The "within" ceaselessly becomes the "without," and man's character is an ever shifting quantum from moment to moment. There is a gain or loss in keeping with the nature of his thoughts, of his emotions, of the words he has spoken or the acts he has committed.

The average man allows himself to become the plaything of his own impulses and addictions. Whims, desires and lusts turn him round and round. The world drives him, and he becomes a creature of chance and circumstance, passing his existence in a heedless state. He judges "good" and "bad," "right" and "wrong" in a narrow, rigid manner. His view is partial, colored by his fantasies and illusions. Often he does things in a mean and thoughtless way.

A man gifted by nature may yet squander his talent and live a heedless life, unmindful of what is expected of him. The higher the talent and the more brilliant the man is, the more powerful are his feelings and drives. If he does not give conscious direction to his overflowing energy, he wrecks his life and leaves behind regrets.

Only the wise man or "Sage," as the Chinese call him, sees the far-reaching influence for good or bad of his thoughts, emotions and of his acts and how he himself is molded by the countless details of his conduct day by day. He takes care to do small things greatly. He does not regard anything that is necessary as unimportant. He has attained full individuality, and, in the truest sense, is master of his destiny. His life radiates light and harmony.

In the words of Lao-Tzu, the ancient chinese philosopher and poet of Taoism, or "the Way:"

> He who stands on his tiptoes does not stand firm; he who stretches his legs does not walk.
> He who displays himself does not shine.
> He who asserts his own views is not distinguished.
> He who vaunts himself does not find his merit acknowledged.
> He who is self-conceited has no superiority allowed to him.
> Such conditions, viewed from the standpoint of the Tao, are like remnants of food, or a tumor on the body, which all dislike.
> Hence, those who pursue the course of the Tao do not adopt and allow them.
>
> - *Tao Te Ching* (James Legge, trans.)

We all live our lives according to what our being is. As is our level of understanding, so is our particular response to life and all its events. Our life is what it is as long as we remain what we are, *as we are.* Unless we change, nothing will change for us. Most of us are not satisfied with the circumstances of our life, but we find hardly anything wrong with ourselves. We do not realize what it means to work on our being, or even why we should.

We, most of us, obey the laws out of fear. We do not feel any other check, and if we were left to ourselves, we would find ourselves behaving in a quite impossible manner, for we have no goodness in us, as a result of the way and manner we have spent our lives.

Spirit can act only in an atmosphere of freedom. Faith and courage are its prime elements, for without these, one cannot lead a life conceived by the spirit. To the eye of the spirit, things happen because they have to happen. Truth comes through an inner light alone. We live in a world of qualitative differences. This means the raising of something lower into the raising of something higher. As we exist in actuality, our exterior life is in miserable discord with our inner life, and our exterior life controls our interior life.

A man may have had a hard and bitter life, leaving in him certain undesirable traits. For him to evolve, he has first to root them out, and this might prove formidable if he has, as it were, petrified.

A man can reach the deep and central ground of his being through his own understanding and effort. Only then can he withstand the pressure of outer things, their pull and their thrust. No lecture, no sermon, no book can normally change a man. Only his own conscious labor, will and understanding can bring about a transformation in him. Were this not so, the world would have changed long ago, what with all the modern means of transmission of knowledge.

We cannot take knowledge about man, his situation and his potentialities in an ordinary way or consider these of no earthly use because it does not conform to our notions of things and their values.

Truly, man has been given many things to ease the days of his life, but he misuses them all. The bounties of nature are so ruthlessly and heartlessly squandered that this planet may become uninhabitable. Man may awake too late, only to discover he has lost everything to make life worth anything. He is much too heedless to regulate the resources of Providence in a proper and thoughtful manner. In ordinary life, no matter what the conditions are, man avoids, if he can, all discomforts and unpleasantness. On a broader level, how negligent and careless he is!

Man can carry out one and the same action differently. He can live through one and the same event differently. Everything hinges upon his inner attitude. Wrong attitudes pile up for him innumerable problems and difficulties.

Man has to realize that if he makes a change in his attitude to an event or to an act, its character will also change. To the awakened man, life is his teacher, testing him in all manner of ways. His approach is alert, sensitive and ever mindful of the flowing consequences of his responses. He is aware that all things in the world have their own particular fate and follow their own natural courses. He tries to distinguish between the surface meaning of things and their inner reality. A very important element of his attitude is his effort to "distance" himself from the events and objects of his perception. This detachment of his is not an end itself but a part of a dynamic interchange with the world around him. He is aware the intrusion of the false "I" would cause a wrong approach. He tries to act without being attached to the fruits of his actions. As a result of this approach, he performs rightly and brings about the right results.

There is no conflict between work and wisdom. The ages of Faith were the ages of master works of creative art, for the craftsman, the artist, and the architect were dedicated to a conscious way of living, and—in their utter devotion—they preferred to remain anonymous.

It is the approach to work, the attitude we bring to it, that makes all the difference in the end result. As the American writer Nathaniel Hawthorne phrases it in his story "The Artist of the Beautiful," "the reward of all high performance must be sought within itself, or sought in vain." **Be it ordinary work or creative, if we go to it without selfish motive or false notions of our worth, it will bring marvelous satisfaction in personal terms, something we had never imagined, and more things will fall in their proper places as of themselves. Selfish motives and false notions of our worth cause havoc in the affairs of daily life and spoil all human relationships. The evil consequences appear like a snowball, growing bigger and bigger as it rolls forward.**

Human destiny is wrapped up in human motive and human sense of worth. It is the manifestation of man's character as it unfolds in history. Man himself is history, yet how appalling his history has been!

CHAPTER 4

Psychic Centers in Man

A feeling has meaning. A thought has meaning. A sensation has meaning. A movement has meaning. These meanings are all different, one from the other.

Man's real life is lived in the psychological sphere: in the cultivation of genuine feeling, clear perception, real insight and true understanding.

It is one thing to *feel* a situation and quite another to *think* about it. There are many things which can only be understood with one's heart and not with one's mind. There is a culture of the heart which is the source of intuition, inspiration and revelation. Education of the emotions and education of the mind have to proceed together for the heart and the head to function in unison. Only then is there a proper and balanced development of man. Paradoxically, they cancel each other out more often than not.

Everyone sees things differently and can see the same things differently at different moments, so that the meanings of things continue to change. This entails that a person's intelligence is made up of many shades of intelligence which connect with different meanings of the same thing.

There are seven Psychic Centers in man. 1. the Instinctive Center; 2. the Moving Center; 3. the Sex Center; 4. the Emotional Center; 5. the Intellectual Center; and, the two higher centers: 6. the higher Emotional Center; and, 7. the higher Intellectual Center.

The higher Emotional Center and the higher Mental Center are potentially so well developed as to be capable of working to their highest capacity in us at all times.

The brain houses the Intellectual Center and the solar plexus the Emotional Center. The spinal cord is the region of the Moving and the Instinctive Centers. These Centers share much in common, just as each Center has its own characteristic work and function.

It is fatal to divide the unitary nature of life, as Descartes did, into separate compartments, into mind and body, unrelated to one another. The distinctions we make between the Centers are just expressions, at various levels, of differing facets of a single, indivisible living organism.

Each Center has a different intelligence and requires a different kind of energy and time-scale. All the Centers present a different relationship of meaning, each in their unique ways, to the same thing. Each Center opens on to a different level of the world.

The Instinctive Center is related to organic life, while the Mental Centers refers to Cosmic Life. We cannot, however, establish any contact with the higher Mental and the higher Emotional Centers, or receive their marvelous vibrations as the other Centers in us are malfunctioning most of the time. As an example, the ordinary Emotional Center is choked with useless, negative feelings.

If we were to take a simple idea and try to look at it from the different Centers, it would present a different facet in each. The more conscious parts are the Emotional and the Intellectual Centers. We pay too much attention to the Moving and the Instinctive Centers, while all the while tragically neglecting to make the right use of the Emotional and the Intellectual Centers. We waste our time on small things. What time, then, could we spare for a meaningful life?

The slowest in speed is the Mental Center and the fastest, the Emotional Center. The Moving and the Instinctive Centers are much faster than the Mental Center, and yet they both have much the same speed.

This means each Center has its own different time and a different speed of function. Why must we then seek miracles in the exterior world to convince ourselves how wondrous God's work is?

Aside from the Emotional Center, the other Centers have positive and negative parts in them. Within the Mental Center reside, *Eemaan* (Affirmation or Faith) and *Kuf'r* (Negation), "yes" and "no." The negative part is as useful in its proper context and function as the positive, and any imbalance between the negative and the positive will lead to mental disorders and psychiatric troubles.

In the Instinctive Center, the two parts may be described as "pleasant" and "unpleasant." There are pleasant sensations of taste, smell, touch, heat or cold and fresh air, indicating conditions of sound health. Unpleasant sensations of touch, bad taste, foul smells, oppressive heat or numbing cold all go to show states injurious to health and disturb the proper functioning of the human organism.

There can be no true orientation in life in the absence either of the positive or the negative: that is "affirmation" or "negation," the "pleasant" or the "unpleasant." Any lack of orientation is a sign of danger to the health of man.

In the Moving Center, "movement" is opposed to "rest" and "rest" to "movement." Both are absolutely necessary.

In the Emotional Center, strange as it may seem, there is no natural "negative" part. Man is born innocent, untainted, unblemished, as is the teaching of Islam. Negative emotions are a grey, blind reaction induced by "imagination" and "identification." Man is subject to many sorrows, grief, fears and anxieties, which are as much a part of his life as are disease, pain and death. These are mental and physical in nature—what we rather know as negative emotions. Now man's Life is over-shadowed by negative emotions which cover the full spectrum of his life's existence. It is as if thick layers of dark clouds shut him off from light. Yet as clouds, no matter how dark and threatening, clear up and leave no trace, negative emotions are just as furtive and disappear the moment "imagination" and "identification" stop. Were they an intrinsic part of the Emotional Center, man would not be able to evolve to higher states of conscious life.

Negative emotions have their own history. They go back to man's childhood. Example and Imitation are the prime causes of the child acquiring negative emotions. He observes his parents and relations and others telling lies, talking ill of one another, cheating and behaving falsely and unpleasantly with others. He stores all these damaging impressions in his psyche, and—as he grows up—he takes in more and more of this disagreeable and infernal negativity from his companions, books, magazines, films, radio, television, the Internet and other corrupting media. One thing marks out negative feelings.

There is no restraint in their expression, as if man were held tight in the vice of an evil power, which would not let him go.

Even his so-called "positive" emotions, such as love, affection, sympathy and the like, can turn at any moment into negative emotions, such as jealousy, envy, hatred, anger, irritation, indignation, pride, vanity and frustration.

These tendencies in man have led to many philosophical and religious explanations, yet the basic truth is what Islam has taught mankind: Man has come into the world with a pure being and essence, and whatever subsequently happens to him to produce all of these evil tendencies is primarily caused by "imagination" and "identification."

How else, then, would it be possible to explain the rise of man to higher states of conscious life, characterized by abiding love, compassion and the higher mental end—all emotional stations in his evolutionary journey?

Most important to the body is the Instinctive Center, which controls the entire internal work of the organism. If its intelligence were interfered with, the whole work of the organism would be under no direction, and that would be fatal to man's very existence.

Centers borrow energy from one another or even steal it. When we fall sick, we feel lassitude, meaning our energy ebbs away. This signifies the Instinctive Center has borrowed energy from the Moving Center. We want simply to rest. If the condition persists, energy is drained from the Emotional Center. We become much quieter and feel no desire to be bothered with things. When it goes to the Intellectual Center, we become aware, we cannot concentrate on anything. In grave illness, the Emotional Center acquires a clearer and deeper intelligence, because "identifying" with objects ceases. Seriously ill or dying persons sometimes show extraordinary insight into things. Such intimations, Wordsworth notes, arise

> Out of human suffering;
> In the faith that looks through death...
> ("Ode to Intimations of Immortality
> from Recollections of Early Childhood")

This has nothing to do with thinking as thinking goes, but there is a process of very deep perception into the nature of things.

Man tends to mix up the energy of the various Centers. He may use the emotional energy to run the mind or the mental energy to drive the Moving Center, or the emotional and mental energy to excite the Sexual Center.

When a person drives a car or plays an instrument or does cycling, for example, he carries out the basic action, without what we know as "thinking." This means the Moving Center is active without the interference of the Mental Center.

To employ an anecdote, there was once a dart player who threw his darts quickly and accurately. A friend asked him how he managed this skill. The dart player, struck by the question, began to observe himself throwing darts. He found he could not let go of the dart in the act of throwing it. The proper functioning of his Moving Center had been interfered with in the act of observation.

The combination of voluntary and reflex actions enables man to survive the dangers he may have to encounter in life.

The Emotional Center, the Mental and the Moving Centers all tend *to steal* energy from the Sexual Center for their own purposes.

The Emotional Center can *see*, the quality of a person, while the Mental Center has to think about it. What a difference there is, in coming to an assessment of the person!

When the Emotional and Mental Centers work in harmony, thinking is very quiet and lucid.

In the Mental Center there is what may be termed, for want of a better word, the "mechanical" segment. Clichés take the place of real thinking. In the Emotional Center, instead of real emotions, the "mechanical" segment may indulge in spurious feelings, expressions of "likes" and "dislikes," all on a superficial level.

We spend most of our time in these "lower segments." Witness our preoccupation with small talk, gossip, scandal, unhealthy curiosities and a thousand other mean feelings and thoughts.

If all the Centers were to function in balance and harmony, everything would then be seen in many different ways and our life would be touched by the eternal. The higher powers, in effect, would be guiding us.

If we can grasp that the higher speed of working of a Center means expanded time and lower speed means contracted time, it may help us to realize that our experience of "time" is relative to our state. Our "time" contains many levels of time. Seen from the higher

Centers, the whole of one's life can be a "moment" in the higher Cosmic Scale, and yet, paradox though it is, each moment of one's life can be a whole life.

When a Center is working at great speed, we experience the paradox of feeling things moving very fast and very slowly, all at the same time. It may seem an eternity before our car hits the other car, and yet it is all over in the twinkling of an eye.

In looking at any problem, if we were to observe deeply, we shall find that we see it differently at different moments. The cause is, the shifting kaleidoscope of "I's."

Man does not know his own limitations nor is he aware of his own possibilities. He does not know who he is, what he is or where he is. He is not aware of himself as he is. The dark side in us is not only what we refuse to admit about ourselves but also what we refuse to utilize. Each Center is really a "mind" giving quite a different aspect and meaning. These aspects and meanings make a whole, infused with cosmic significance. How necessary it is, then, to cultivate new interests and develop new insights and a deeper understanding to evolve to higher levels of being.

We spend most of our time in a vague, unfocused state in which a stream of mechanical inner talking and phantasies flow on unceasingly. This is living between the Centers.

To know with the mind and to know with the heart are worlds apart. Merely to think when one should also feel is wrong and merely to feel when one should also think is equally wrong. Acting without thinking and feeling is also wrong.

We have within us an untapped wealth of new ground, but people prefer to walk the same beaten paths. After a certain age, they are nothing but a rag-bag of acquired habits in every Center.

If a person desires to evolve into a balanced man, it is imperative for him to have a positive, normal attitude to sex and respect for its healthy expression. Nothing abnormal or negative should ever be allowed to touch it. Yet to make use of a person of either sex to satisfy one's lust is to be guilty of the most serious moral turpitude. The person will have closed himself to all higher development. Some use their sex for self-glorification, but this increases their inner uneasiness. When an action is mixed with self-glory, one's life becomes spurious.

By its inherent nature, sex is the most private activity of man. Yet it has been blatantly exploited and exhibited by purveyors of "free sex." Lechery leads to the basest conduct. On the other extreme, inhibition in sex has led to morbidities. They are all states which alienate man from himself and throw him into extreme imbalance, making it difficult for him even to remain normal and maintain his human dignity.

Those who do not have the right attitude towards sex tend to treat that very fine, delicate and essential quality "shame" lightly, as if it were of no consequence. Yet if we take away the natural sense of shame, what is left of man?

A natural sense of shame is the most intimate part of sex, and it is also the root of religion. Islam therefore, puts particular emphasis on shame as an integral part of human conduct.

A quote from the Islamic tradition has much to teach us of man's psychic center and his *telos* or purpose:

> These meanings do not concern the
> negligent man, nor the transitory man nor
> the man of wrong action nor the man who
> follows his whims.
>
> > -Al-Hallaj, *Tawasin*

Turning from the Islamic to the Christian tradition, different meanings and psychic centers troubled Augustine as he turned from a worldly life to a religious life, for he began to question everything around him, asking the "who" and what" of his very self and how God, whom he had not heeded, stood behind all:

> I have become a problem [question] to
> myself.
>
> > — Augustine, *Confessions*, Book X,
> > Caput 33 (E. B. Pusey, trans.)

In *Varieties of Religious Experience*, William James is perhaps right to speak of Augustine's "change" in psyche and to discuss him as an example of a "divided self," but divisions and separate aspects of the self may be more holistic than is commonly supposed. It should be noted at this point there are four aspects in man's soul, which is called *un-Nafs*—the blissful soul or the commanding soul. There also is the ego-centered soul, driving man relentlessly to pursue his egotistic impulses and inclinations. He is impelled to commit evil acts, ranging the entire spectrum. He is dragged down to the basest and the most heinous crimes. In the process, he sheds off all his humanity and degenerates into a veritable Mephistopheles, the fitting symbol of negation.

The accusing soul, as it is termed most appropriately, is that aspect of the soul which warns and alerts him, in moments of awareness lest he may fall into the trap of wrong decisions and acts. The fusion of consciousness and conscious turns him back to truth and upright conduct. The blissful soul is in complete harmony with man's spirit and rests in a state of certainty and bliss. The fourth aspect relates to instincts and tendencies common between man and animals. This aspect is passively obedient to natural instincts and tendencies. The Holy Qur'an states that man will testify against his own Nafs soul on the day of judgement. (76:14) Al-Ghazali has pointed out that it is not thought, nor perception, nor Imagination but will through which man comes to realize his spiritual possibilities. Man is free in his will. This is the psychical and sensuous world where relative freedom is recognized and human will is exercised. Al-Ghazali equates the tendencies of Nafs-soul with spiritual diseases. Some of these include Hypocrisy, Arrogance, Impulses, Avarice, and Ghafla, an obsessive pre occupation with things of this world. This leads to superficiality and levity and then to licentiousness and vulgarity. There is ostentatious display and leads inevitability to callousness and indifference to others plight and suffering – a lust for power concupiscence.

CHAPTER 5

Essence and Personality

"Essence" is that with which a man is born, and "personality" is that which he acquires in life. Personality is thus the sum total of all the various influences that shape him into what he is, especially his environment and education. Rarely is there a right development of "personality." Man's milieu turns him egocentric. Yet ask him, and he will deny he is egocentric. No matter what he may really be, he carries a good opinion of himself. There is no end to man's delusions, deceptions and imaginings about what he is.

In the child, the "essence" is active. In the adult, and specifically in the man who is awake, "personality" recesses and essence are activated.

All efforts at self-development hinge upon the growth of "essence" and a very conscious inner state.

Since "essence" is active in the child, he truly lives in the moment, and is only concerned with the essential and intrinsic nature of the objects he perceives around him. His sensory life, unlike that of the adult, is extremely rich. His gaze is innocent, and he does not differentiate between himself and the object, nor does he draw any comparison or contrast between one object and another. To him, the object is not separate from him. Subject and object are one, fused in the act of perception itself, which is therefore unitary in character.

"Earth fills her lap with pleasures of her own... And with new joy and pride, the little actor cons another part," writes Wordsworth in reflecting on the transition from early childhood to being influenced by the world. As the child grows into an adult, the world exerts all kinds of influence upon him, with the result that he recedes from his "essence" and comes to wear the mask of "personality," which is at best a dubious asset, and he dies, still donning the mask. He lives in a state of duality and sees himself and others through the distorting lenses of his "personality." To him, subject and object stand opposite to each other, the seer and the seen are alien. He has already lost the faculty of what may be called "bare," "naked" attention, which is a marvelous faculty. He is a total stranger to "pure perception," which is possessed by the child—the great artist, mystic, and—in Wordsworth's term – "Nature's priest." He cannot see any object without the colored glasses of "associative thinking," attempting to recall similar objects or making comparisons and contrasts with other objects of his experience. He becomes incapable of apprehending any object such as it is, in its dynamic reality.

Pure perception has no trace whatsoever of associative thinking. The eye becomes so highly sensitized as to be able to register the symbols of the universal. A profound mystic feeling enters into the experience, a feeling of identity and unity with reality itself. This is the state of the great poet, the sage, the saint and—not to be neglected, the authentic lover. The man becomes both the observer and the observed. This feeling may come in moments of an extreme situation or near death.

A leaf, a blade of grass or any common object is then seen and endowed with properties unique to itself. Man can recapture the seraphic gleam, the vision and innocence of childhood. Yet he transcends the child and stands at a much higher conscious level. This is an excellent example of the spiral character of a self–evolutionary *leap*. As in the child, the "essence" is once again active, and the man's egocentric personality fades away.

It is extraordinary what an "egocentric personality" does to a man. He may go to the ends of the earth, even to outlandish places. Yet he would still be carrying with him all the acquired habits of his life and thought. On his return, he would still be his old self, and hardly anything would have changed in him. When relating or recalling his experiences of men and places, his old habits of life and thought would still be stamped upon them. Even a constant change of environment can become a mechanical exercise, like everything else.

We shall never learn to live a conscious life if we do not work on our "personality" and see what troubles are caused by our own selves and not by others. Yet we imagine it is very much worth possessing a "personality," with all its labels and medals. We strut about imagining we are praised and admired and say to ourselves what "wonderful chaps" we are. This is sheer self-deception, and our attitude is yet a further example of the disharmony of being in us.

On the other hand, if a man suffers from a profound sense of inferiority and is going through a crisis, self-pity takes possession of him, and he moans and howls at his fate. This is another example of disharmony of being within the man.

The world is rich in examples of this terrible lack of grounding in the center of man's being as a result of his egocentric personality. There are harsh, narrow judgments and tight, fixed attitudes "imprisoning" him, never letting him realize what is actually wrong with him.

Fear and anxiety set in when a man tries to keep up what is not genuine in him. He lives in a constricted part of himself, and the rest is dark to him. He is not open to his own self, nor is he open to others without deception or evasion and excuses. There is an infinite capacity in man to disguise the harsh and bitter truths about himself and to believe he is doing one thing, when in fact he is doing something very different. Unconsciously, he uses cunning dodges which only go to hide from him the true condition of his inner state. The more respectable these subtle stratagems seemingly appear, the more dishonest and dangerous they are. Self-deception, evasions and excuses make him the prisoner of his own phantasies. They cause a great strain on his being and lead to moral aridity, boredom and psychic suffering. At the heart of self-deception, there lurks a terrible egoism—the "web and woof" of an egocentric personality.

If you seek a Pharisee, go to an egocentric personality. It protects itself in conventional rituals of behavior and ever pretends to be what it is not. A secret anxiety and nervousness gnaw at him and never give him peace or tranquility. He persists in nursing the illusion that others are struck and impressed by him and that he is a successful man of the world. Let the situation change for him, and all the props that held and sustained him would fall and he would collapse like a burst balloon.

The man who is free from an egocentric personality is flexible like a green twig, able to bend with the storm, capable of adapting himself in the right manner to whatever may come to pass, whether good or bad.

To be amongst persons who have shed their egocentric personality is to experience a fresh new world where the atmosphere is pure and radiant.

CHAPTER 6

Knowledge, Being and Understanding

> He giveth - wisdom unto whom He will,
> and he unto whom wisdom is given,
> he truly hath received abundant good.
> But none remember except men of
> understanding.
>
> - Holy Qur'an (2:269)

A man's life is conditioned by the conditioning of his desires. They mold him and set the direction he will take. As long as he cannot free himself from this bind, he will never be able to think beyond himself and his desires. He will swing back and forth between desire and its satisfaction, between personal grievances and personal advantages. This is a selfish and conceited life.

Each one of us, such as he is, has a level of being and a level of knowledge, on a scale of understanding. Understanding, therefore, is the crux of human life. The Qur'an says: "Say: This is my way. I call unto God on the basis of understanding." (12: 108)

"Being" is the psyche of man in its totality, consisting of all the good, bad and indifferent elements that make him what he is.

A human-being can develop in two directions only: one is knowledge, and the other is "being." In knowledge, quality matters most. Knowledge is of many kinds. The more a man is able to discriminate between knowledge and being, the better he is able to place himself and develop his sense of being and understanding. Knowledge and being have to be fused to create understanding. The more a man understands, the higher his being will be. To understand is to set-up a right and proper relationship to all things that come under purview. It was Leonardo da Vinci who stated, "To understand is to set up a relationship."

It is not the size of a man, his strength, his money, his power, or his status that really describes him. He is in reality his own, Understanding, and the ultimate realization of himself is: A man's understanding is *what he is*.

We will this or we will that. What matters most, is to *will*, what we know. If we do not *will*, our "knowledge," then our being will not fuse with what we know. Whether knowledge outpaces being or being outgrows knowledge, two consequences follow: 1) our development will remain lop-sided; 2) there will be some deep inner contradiction to harass our life.

In our ordinary state, we do not *will* what we know. We have to realize that we act from our level of being, not from our level of knowledge. Our "will" issues in action, and our "will" arises in our being. The result is that we are able to see "the better" we follow "the worse" in our action. Quite clearly, knowledge and being have not interfused. As long as this continues to be our state, we shall have no unity in ourselves and very little understanding.

Man's being is very complex. We see persons whose intellectual growth is exceptional, and yet in their emotions, they appear desiccated. They are developed in one part only and there, too, only up to a point. They can truly be said to be lop-sided. They are said *to know*, but they are incapable of *applying* what they know to what they will to do. They break down when they have to face difficulties. Their level of being is, as a result, below their level of knowledge. They hear the word, but they cannot apply the word to the act. Clearly there is a paralysis of *will*. Knowledge remains theoretical. They cannot overcome their doubts and their hesitations, and their approach is not able to break out of its negativity.

To impel us in the right direction, knowledge must be suffused with emotion. An intellectual man tends to distort life. He is always trotting out rational explanations, which may be dry as dust and incapable of catching the delicate nuances of an emotionally vibrant situation. He cannot *feel* persons or situations. Dissecting things is all he knows, and thus he fails to show understanding. What a terrible deficiency that is!

How is it that a man could "experience" above his level of being? This is due to the fact that the level at which he stands is really a composite of slightly higher and lower layers, on which lie his better "I's" and worse "I's." Yet taken altogether, his level is mechanical, in the sense there is absent from that very essential thing a proper degree of awareness or consciousness. All the same, at different psychological moments his level is characterized by lower or higher degrees of mechanicalness. This makes it possible for the man to "experience" beyond his particular level of being. In other words, his "receptive" side is better than his "doing" side.

In certain situations, we do get a flash of insight in which we see what it is that we must "do," and yet find ourselves unable just to "do" that. This is due to the lack of unity in the states of our being, knowledge and understanding. They do not occupy the same level. We have to realize that we cannot be other than what are, just as others cannot be any different from what they are. We move on different wave lengths.

Knowledge need not necessarily bring understanding. Understanding should be equated neither with knowledge nor with being. Only when knowledge and being become interfused and intertwined is understanding born. Once understanding comes, it remains, because its essential quality is that it is the child of the union of being and knowledge. For this very reason, understanding can never be borrowed. Once it has come to us, it will never be lost.

All inner development of man depends upon understanding. It is not possible to compel a man to understand. He sees the truth of a thing, or he does not. To argue is not to understand, and to understand is not to argue. What is genuine in a man is beyond all quarreling and argument. The higher the understanding, the finer, the subtler and the deeper the meanings of objects revealed.

Man is created to be so unique that no two persons could ever share the same kind of being. In the psychological sense, the real neighbor of a person is another person who is nearest to him in his level of being. They will draw to each other as there is bound to be some affinity between them. All around us we find people who have divergent tastes and interests. They are fond of an infinite variety of things, each in his own individual way, choosing what suits his taste. Only those sharing similar tastes will be drawn towards one another, and they are therefore psychological neighbors.

One way to escape from the "imperious" demands of self-conceit is to seek one's own psychological neighbor. Shared things counteract the effects of self-idolatry, which is a self-imposed bondage.

A person's meaning of things will correspond to the level of being to which he belongs. He will not ever be able to understand beyond the level of his being. His understanding will accord to his level. It will not correspond to the meaning of things. He can be taught many things, yet all the effort will lead to nothing, until his level of being is raised to agree with that knowledge.

What Man *is* depends on what the level of his being is. He is what his disposition is. Man comes to know himself only through his acts, not through "thinking" about himself. The acts of man betray all the tendencies he unconsciously harbors within himself. He may spend all his life "thinking" what he is, yet he will never arrive at the truth of himself. The moment he acts, he begins to reveal what he actually is, for an "act" is a terrible exposer. Yet it is possible that with an act, a man may dissemble, yet at some point all dissemblers are exposed.

We have an illusion that if we were to change our outward form of life, we would change our being. The exact opposite is true. Our life changes only when our being changes. An "outward" oriented man will find this difficult to understand. We do not see that we have distinct and limited outlines of character. We imagine we are free and boundless. We believe we can be anything we want or do anything we may please and live how we would choose. These are illusions about ourselves. Reality is very different. The harsh truth is we are limited and confined to what our particular beings are, and we cannot be other than what we are. Only a very hard and consistent effort of changing our being will release us from our present state and lead us to a higher level, freer and less confined than before.

We have a tendency to delude ourselves into believing that we are what we actually are not and that we are not what we actually are. How treacherous our delusions about ourselves! In our state, is it ever possible to take one step forward towards self-evolution? We cannot truly see our own life from the level of being at which we are situated.

The less we can tolerate, the lower our being is. We cannot forgive or forget, for we see our own merit. Besides humans, there are communities of living things with their uncanny, unerring sense of direction which have their own intelligent spheres of being in which their communal life moves: The migratory birds, bees, ants, seals, herds of animals on the plains and savannas, fish which make astonishing migrations in the breeding season, insects and bats in caves, and numerous other creatures on land, sea and air, all with their territorial instincts. The Holy Qur'an says: "There is not an animal in the earth, nor a flying creature flying on two wings, but they are peoples like unto you. We have neglected nothing in the Book (of our Decrees)." (6:38)

Every man's being has an attribute that is peculiar to him alone. He may be like a hawk or a vulture, a fox or a hyena, and the condition of his soul will be akin to the nature of that creature. Even his face may resemble it.

Some faces are "horsy," some "foxy," some "leonine," some "bovine," and the "game" of naming could continue *ad infinitum*. Yet these are not at all amusing caricatures to make us laugh, for there is a sad commentary here on what man has reduced himself to as a result of his undeveloped spiritual condition.

There has been an age-old tendency encouraged by all religions with the exception of Islam to run away from the world, retire to a monastery, go to a cave in the mountains or seek sanctuary in the depths of a forest. The idea is to escape from the pull and glitter of the world, and to change one's "being" in isolation by "force." This is really not getting rid of the world in such an artificial manner. All such efforts are misleading. It is an affront to man's destiny in the scheme of cosmic life to withdraw from his responsibilities as a sojourner on Earth to retreat into an unaccounted life, for to live in the world is to hold oneself accountable. Islam has therefore forbidden monastic life for man. While it is true that the Prophet Muhammad, peace be upon him, was himself on a solitary desert retreat outside of Mecca, this was before prophethood. After the first revelation (Holy Qur'an, 74:1-2), it is notable that the notion of retreating from the world ended, for Islam teaches man to discharge to the limit his responsibilities and duties as a person moving in the thick of life At the same time, man must try his utmost not to become too worldly in the process.

If we could see our being through a spiritual vision, we would be able to observe clearly that certain elements in it have led to all the troubles that happened to us. If we had no inner life and were suddenly wrenched from all that we valued and took pride in, we would be crushed.

Having nothing else in us, we would collapse under the vision of a higher level and another order of things. If we were to find ourselves without any personal effort at a level of being above our own, we would feel lost. We would not know what it would mean to be living on that level. No one, therefore, can outstrip his own level of being.

There are degrees of reality in which we pass our lives. The higher the level of our being, the deeper is our reality and the freer we are. The lower it is, the more bound we are and the more tenuous our reality is. All our significance as "man" consists in our becoming authentic persons, possessing unity and wholeness. Else we shall remain "unreal," fragmented, unfree and mechanical, enmeshed in self-deceptions and lies all of our lives.

Complaining and grousing on events and things are most common among us. Yet a man of higher being never complains or expresses negative feelings. He is completely free from negative attitudes.

We grow through our own understanding not by being told what to do. The change in us comes through *seeing* with an inner eye what we have to do and *realizing* what our being actually is.

Our understanding alters as our being alters. Mechanical thinking and mechanical feeling merely limit our being, and we continue to whirl round and round a "dead" circle of habits.

In essence, persons of different levels of being cannot come together. How can they? After all, different categories belong to different levels of understanding. A higher intelligence could never be comprehensible to a lower one.

A person may be very clever; he may be outstanding in his field of work. Yet he may not be conscious of anything higher. His being stays at a lower level, and yet we continue to commit the error of imagining that a very clever or brilliant person must have a high level of being. Neither Herod nor Pilate, occupying the highest positions in life, were fit to receive the esoteric teaching of Christ. The most tragic thing is when a man of low being comes into power, he attracts all that belongs to his level of being. He spreads terror and misery, and life becomes unendurable.

There is a category of persons who call themselves "religious." These are the ones who follow the letter and ignore the spirit. They imagine that, with their appalling "self-righteousness," shot through with negative emotions, vanity, malicious talking and unpleasant curiosity, they would go to paradise. There are many such illusions, and they are due to not "seeing" (i.e., "perceiving") their level of being. They become distorted in the negative side of human character.

People make all sorts of useless efforts to attain "enlightenment." They practice asceticism, torture their bodies, keep vows of silence, starve themselves, deny themselves even innocent pleasures, repeat endless prayers mechanically and do unpleasant and unreasonable things. These practices merely turn them into hard, inflexible persons, with no real change in their being. Their approach shows a deficient understanding and intelligence and does not give any results. They have to realize that without undergoing some stage of *metanoia*, nothing could change their being, which is really the first step to ascend to higher levels of being.

What one man may need at a certain time may be quite different from what another man may need at that very moment. We all have our individualities and idiosyncrasies, and therefore our requirements will differ. A single effort of inner sincerity can shift our position and lift us to a higher level of being. Nothing false or half-hearted can achieve any good.

All development of being is in the direction of the increasing union of our outer and inner selves, and the end is the unity of being. Only then do we come to possess full consciousness and will, free from all whims, caprices and accidents, impervious to any pressure or change directed from "without."

The philosopher Albert Pike makes this insightful statement about being in its truest sense:

> What is certain, even for science and the reason, is, that the idea of God is the grandest, the most holy, and the most useful of all the aspirations of man; that upon this belief morality reposes, with its eternal sanction. This belief, then, is in humanity, the most real of the phenomena of *being* [...]
>
> (*Morals and Dogma*, Chapter 3; emphasis by the editor)

The man in contact with God is the one whose knowledge and being are both at their highest level and so equal that all his understanding is practical. Such a man was the Prophet Muhammad, peace be upon him.

Religion consists in "doing." A man must live his religion as fully as is within his power and capacity to live it. Islam's whole emphasis is on Action and Conduct, not on mere outward profession of faith, which is incomplete without the right approach and conduct. Words without action—how they contradict and cancel out one another!

Man fails to understand that religion will be the test of his level of understanding, and his level of understanding will be as his level of being is. We are imprisoned within our own petty selves.

Self-worship is like the blood that circulates through our entire body. Its control and grip is ever so tight and pervasive! Only a violent shock that shakes our entire being to its roots can ever release its terrible hold on us and put us on the path of realization that living is living in the presence of God, a mere caricature and no more, yet full of an inherent dignity, as man in the midst of other men and God's other creatures. We are not what we imagine we are. Our situation is fraught with dangers. We walk on the edge of a steep cliff. Our prevarications, our sliding back, our justifying and seeking refuge in false hopes and spurious reasons put us into sleep amnesia of our real self. How, then, can we ever achieve our redemption? When we have ceased either to condemn or to justify and we are able to accept ourselves as we have been and are at present, it is only then that we are confronted with the harsh truth about ourselves. If we acknowledge sincerely our true situation, then an unusual stillness may come upon us. The narrow self of everyday life can then be transcended, and we are liberated from our own bondage.

CHAPTER 7

Understanding Others

In his "Night Shadows" chapter of *A Tale of Two Cities*, Dickens observes

> that every human creature is constituted to be that profound secret and mystery to every other. A solemn consideration, when I enter a great city by night, that every one of those darkly clustered houses encloses its own secret; that every room in every one of them encloses its own secret; that every beating heart in the hundreds of thousands of breasts there, is, in some of its imaginings, a secret to the heart nearest it!

One of the greatest evils of human relationship is that people make no attempt to enter into one another's position and situation. All they do is carp and criticize. They show no understanding. They have no insight into themselves, their own crudities and shortcomings. As a result, the normal balance of human affairs is badly upset and a leaden psychic atmosphere spoils all the traffic of life. If only people were to see themselves and others simultaneously, they could neutralize the effects of their behavior in daily intercourse.

Man lives on two levels: one where he is absorbed in his own ego, with all its self-deceptions, posturing and delusions; the other where he is the constant object of a merciless scrutiny by others. How others see him is not how he sees or regards himself. There is a flaw at both the levels. The critical appraisal of others may not be able to fathom the complexities of his inner world, his motives and urges, and they may fail to get a rounded view of him. He, covered by veils of self-deceptions and delusions, is unable to see the picture others have of him. He falls into rationalization of his conduct, and the bridge between the two levels remains uncrossed.

We believe that if we condemn and criticize, we do good to others. All we do in fact is to oppress them. It is a miserable failure of understanding. To understand another person, empathy is necessary to probe into his psychological state. This is not possible if we have not probed into our own psychological state. For this, the tool must be "internal attention." In so far as a man knows himself consciously, he will know the other person consciously. This is an objective process, free from all subjective feelings and phantasies. Without being far more conscious of himself, he cannot become conscious of the other person, except in an illusory way.

We have to become aware of our own motives and drives. If we ask ourselves why we do this or say that, write this or that, we actually "undress" ourselves. This self-observation must be free from tension, anxiety, or psychic strain if it is to give us a true picture of things. We have to realize that a great many processes that go on in the mind stop if we try to look at them too directly. This is especially true of the imagination. Self-observation should be like the light of a torch that is flashed into a darkroom. It shows all the objects there without being critical of them. We have to possess a subtle, delicate touch in our probing.

A person may think about himself all day long and yet never observe himself once. How strange that is—and yet how common it is! A man is first one; then, when he "observes" himself, he divides himself in two, the observer and the observed, one indivisible process. At the end of it all, he is again "one," and he has already obtained a complete picture of his psychological state.

Everyone is in a "prison" of himself. To see this, he has to divide himself into two, one active and the other passive, the latter of which stands inside and behind the active side. First, he must observe each thing in himself and reach the point where he is placed to observe himself *altogether*, complete and whole, taking every care not to forget it has to be objective, free from all the taints of a subjective approach. He will come to *notice* all his thoughts and phantasies, all his lies and excuses and private plays. With a shock, he will discover that the person revealed is not he himself, but someone else, a stranger to his ordinary notion of himself. Yet this "stranger" is he himself, fully exposed in all his nakedness.

To learn to know the real from the false and to be able to separate them is not light and easy. Too often we take things to be what they are not in reality. We then live in the unreal and believe the false to be the true. That which deceives us or is illusory in character robs us of reality. The real is always that which gives meaning, worth and significance to life. To lose hold of the real is the death of the spirit. Hell is the irrevocable loss of reality.

The more we see into ourselves, the more we can see into other people. If we are blind to ourselves, we will be blind to others never be able to understand them.

Understanding is the most powerful force we can create in ourselves. As we see through ourselves, we shall see through the tricks and lies of others. Strangely, this will free us from their power. It is standing too high up in ourselves and feeling superior that puts us so often under their power. We are then no longer surprised and indignant with them. We cannot take a person to be simply what our opinion of him is or what he is reputed to be in life. A relationship with people demands much care and attention. It is how we behave *internally* and *invisibly* with others that matters most. We must handle a person we are working with as carefully and as consciously in our *inner thoughts*, as we behave externally out of polite manners. Our common failing is we do not treat others well in inter-personal relationships. We are most often negative with them, as we are negative with most affairs of external life. If we were not so negative and had the right attitude, we would not be in bondage to one another. For example, if a man's whole happiness depends on one person alone, then he becomes a function of that person, and that damages human dignity. The tragedy is we often allow ourselves to become mere tools of others and permit them to "use" us for their own ends—the most awful thing we can do to murder our human dignity and respect. Man is no slave to anyone, but he slides into slavery for various reasons and in various circumstances. He forfeits to call himself a man, vicegerent of God on earth, though he is His creature, according to the teaching of Islam. This is consistent with his vicegerency, for he is a created being.

Empathy and sympathy are inter-related. The real meaning of sympathy is to "feel with" the other person. In the sentimental sense, "sympathy" is false, as it is mixed with conceit and condescension. If we want to help, we must *feel* as he *feels*, through empathy and understanding. Many pretend they have goodwill towards others. Outwardly they are civil and polite with them, but within they may despise and detest them. There are a hundred things that may prevent a man from expressing his true feelings.

Most of us are too much under the very subtle and pleasant influence of our fancies to register any distinct facts about ourselves. If we are mean and hypocritical, we do not see ourselves that way. In any case, others seem to us to be the mean and hypocritical ones, not we. How soothing self-deception is!

A man has moral arrogance and yet looks at it as a virtue, that he was, God be thanked, not "like the others." Again, how marked by self-deception!

We think we do not do the mean and silly things others do. We feel we are better than they are. We are shut out from our own selves, and we cannot *see,* the mean and silly things we often do ourselves. Everyone's way of being mean, silly and foolish is different from others.

We are apt to judge and condemn others who behave in a manner we disapprove; this means we *hate* in secret.

To wound others gives no satisfaction or inner peace. One cold, heartless remark can smash everything, just as a single venomous word can make a person explode into fury.

We must learn to *visualize* our own behavior towards others. This is directed imagination, and an activity demanding tranquility. In our speech, in unguarded moments and in trifles we have not the slightest awareness we give ourselves away.

In general, we put the unconscious side of ourselves into others. We *project* this side of ourselves into them. This means our consciousness extends to a very small part of our own selves. We therefore relate badly related to life, to others, and to ourselves.

The thing a person criticizes so much in others is something lying in the dark side of himself that he does not know and does not acknowledge. What he does not see in himself, he sees reflected in the other persons. If he were to study the persons he dislikes, he would discover projected and unadmitted parts of himself. This would shatter his self-conceit.

Two men who detest each other are, paradoxically, closer to each other emotionally than they could ever have suspected. It is quite possible that they might strike up some sort of a relationship in the end. There is something common between two persons who hate each other, for they hate that in themselves which the other appears to embody. What we condemn most in others is some unadmitted part of our own selves.

Allow a man to give free vent to his feelings about others and we might as well say: "Thou art the man," *Tu quoque.* (2 Samuel 12: 7) The incomparable mystic Persian poet Mawlana Rumi says, "If you perceive a fault in your brother, the fault you perceive in him is within yourself... Get rid of that fault within you, for what distresses you in him distresses you in yourself." (A.J Arberry, trans.) The great sage further observes, "All evil qualities—oppression, hatred, greed, mercilessness, pride—when they are within yourself, do not pain you. When you perceive them in another, then you *shy away,* and are pained."

We must be so mindful as to hold and sustain and not "murder" one another. With the growth of consciousness, we enter a more spacious world and become more universal.

To cheer up a person who is unhappy is ordinary human decency, but we have to listen to the person with our internal ear and find the corresponding state in us. We then make it possible for the man to change his state. This is quite different from helping the person in the ordinary way, which is really the "blind helping the blind."

The more isolated a man is, the less of an individual he will be and the less he would show those qualities which distinguish one man from another. When a man becomes psychotic, it is very hard to establish any kind of relationship with him. The most isolated people in the world are schizophrenics. They are remarkably alike. It is most dangerous for our psyche if, for some reason or other, we get cut off from the stream of life. In a sense, we become "dead." In the absence of relationships, men tend to become more alike, not more various and individualistic. Isolation rubs off all distinctive features and not, as one would suppose, accentuate them. Man is most individual when he is most in contact with other men, and he is least an individual when he is most isolated from them.

To feel completely lonely and isolated is to accelerate mental disintegration. It is like starving oneself to death.

If a person dislikes you, try to observe what it is that he dislikes in you. We must thank those who make it possible for us to work on our self-improvement.

The person who says he is very considerate to others and puts them first in his thoughts may just be deceiving himself. It is not possible to do this without conscious effort.

In seeing others try to observe: How does he take things? What kind of man is he in his dealings with others?

In order to influence others, we have first to know then our inner nature. If we do not work with it, we cannot see it in ourselves or ourselves in it. If we lack this insight, we shall only have a warped opinion of our own value.

Most of our daily intercourse with other people is regulated by social conventions and customs, and they are things which make us shallow and artificial. We fail to treat persons with whom we have dealings as individuals in their own right.

We do not realize that to see selfishness in others is to see the reflection of our own selfishness. The more demands we make on others the more selfish they will appear to us.

It is very painful to realize there is anything wrong with us. We may say we are to blame, but if others agree, we feel hurt and offended. We may pretend we are wrong, but to *see* it in ourselves can be most distressing. This is real suffering. All real suffering is cathartic in nature.

It is not possible for an ordinary man really to put himself in another man's situation. How can he? He is himself mechanical, negative in his emotions, has prejudices, is vain and self-satisfied. He cannot see himself. How then can he see others or their situations?

We think people do things unintentionally, but fail to see they do them mechanically. That is the most common state of man. A man can be very satisfied with his mechanicalness, not that he is aware he is mechanical. He sees it as his own intelligent, conscious self. If anyone were to touch him beneath his outer self, he would find a complacent self-esteem, which is really the explanation of his mechanicalness. Below the surface, he strongly approves of himself. To keep up appearances, he may deprecate himself before others.

A man is related to different sides of himself in different ways. He has to learn to see things at various angles, to see the difficulties of others by putting himself in their place and to see his own difficulties as objectively as possible. Only in this way he will reach a new feeling of himself. His sight will be clearer and will penetrate below the surface. He will possess "more light," to quote Goethe's legendary final words.

We should try not to find fault with others, but bear their unpleasant behavior patiently. We are perhaps just as difficult for others as we feel they are for us. We have to realize how mechanical all of us are. We have first to bear with our own selves before we can bear with others. It acts like a soothing balm to exercise a sense of humor and laugh at our own foibles and idiosyncratic behavior. More than anything, we have to give up having our way all the time. We should be able to eat, drink, talk and listen without showing any trace of superiority. We may have an opportunity to say something striking to impress others, but we should refrain from saying it. There ought to be no hint, conscious or unconscious, of our being above them in our behavior. This is the only way we can put others at ease. After all, what is there so exclusive or precious in us when we clearly see ourselves in others and others in ourselves? This comes as a revelation, blotting out self-idolatry. A true expansion of consciousness is to see ourselves in our neighbors and our neighbors in ourselves. We then begin to understand that the development and extension of this conscious relationship leads us to that compassion for the world that the Prophets of God affirmed in their own lives. This would leave in us a permanent state of insight and understanding with a new feeling of "I." The power of healing will then be ours, like grace from God. We shall then touch to heal and bind a bruised heart, a seared and overwrought mind, the thousand ills from which the heart and mind of man suffer.

CHAPTER 8

Persona and Attitudes

In life, we imitate others, and we are extraordinarily suggestible to what we see, hear or are told. This is the root of the desire to imitate. We form "pictures" of ourselves. Everyone has the "itch" to be like someone he admires or to be something he is not in life. People are not what they imitate or pretend they are. How long is it possible to maintain an artificial state of oneself? How remarkable it is that we human beings do not take as our models the sages and the prophets who have had such a profound and ennobling influence in history! We have to go and imitate popular idols of the moment in sports and on stage and screen—persons who in their private lives show very undesirable traits of character, very far from the models they appear in all their gilt and glitter. The glamour of the world is blinding, and nothing is as attractive and irresistible for the worldlings that we are. We love to live in a world of phantasies and try to avoid the realities of life which are harsh and often hard to endure. We thus seek substitutes and love to lose ourselves in them.

When the Prophet Moses asked God His name, a Voice answered him: "I AM that I AM." (Exodus 3:14)

The man pure in heart would never be other than what he is in himself. To Be is not to fantasize. He IS what he is and no other. This is the core of individuality, the personal self in all its dimensions. Imitation just makes a man unreal. Phantasies about what he feels he looks like or identifies himself with, if allowed to go unchecked, consciously or unconsciously, make it very difficult for him to become an authentic person, for there is no reality in him. He is, in fact, false in his life.

We lead "invented" lives of all sorts, based on "pictures" and "roles." The side of what we are and the side of what we imagine or pretend we are contradict each other. Our internal state is in a very bad condition. The laws and imperatives of life would never permit us to defy them, no matter what our private desires, whims and fancies may be. We feel terribly proud to copy "idols" of our imagination, and we shall pay the price of losing our own personal self in the process. We shall be left vacuous – as it were, with an empty shell.

It is quite an experience to watch a person *active* in some picture, image or "role model" he has changed himself into, and we wonder why he cannot see it. This is very simple. What is not so simple is to discover ourselves in such a "picture." We have no awareness of this tendency in ourselves and are ultimately no different from others, for we all hypnotize our own selves.

A man and a woman fantasize and rush into marriage, believing they will be very happy together. The marriage reveals traits and habits of each which become repugnant to the other. They fly from each other, a disastrous end to the romantic "picture" that so powerfully pulled them to each other. The "plays" we enact lay bare, sooner or later, the ugly truths about ourselves, no matter how desperately we may try to hide them from others. This is reaching a point of no return, and to retrace thence is unimaginably hard. How is it possible to rectify a situation that has run its course?

The genuine and the spurious belong to different orders and stand at different levels, yet we strut about quite satisfied with ourselves enacting our "plays." Nonetheless, we do get caught by things that expose the truth about ourselves. "Pictures" are a source of inner discord and instability. We have a "picture" that we are honest and truthful. If circumstances show us not being honest and truthful, we are thrown into a very uncomfortable situation. We squirm, explain, argue and try to justify ourselves. Yet it would be better to be caught in a wrong act than to go on pretending and justifying. We make it possible to bear the burden of our own failings.

At the same time, we hate to discipline ourselves. Much of the inner work consists in getting rid of undesirable tendencies in us and of stopping impulsive actions, of indulging in private "plays" and of dissolving ourselves in "pictures" which appear so attractive and desirable to us. A self-satisfied man will say, "Why on earth should I try to change myself when I am well placed in the world, comfortable and not lacking in things desired by others? Why should I leave Egypt and go into the wilderness?" We much prefer slavery with security to freedom and dignity with insecurity. What we are depends upon what the world is for us. As we are, so is the world we have created.

If the external side affirms and the internal denies, man is being pulled in opposite directions. This is being divided against his own self. Only an inner realization can destroy the power of a "picture." In a state of self-awareness, no "picture" can have any influence on the man. Yet we all live in some sort of an artificial state. For example, when we talk to a man possessed by a strong "picture," we have a furtive impression he is someone else. Man is very seldom aware of himself as a distinct, throbbing, vital individual. "One man in his time plays many parts [and] roles" in life, as Shakespeare observes in his famous "Seven Ages of Man" monologue in *As You Like It*. Man changes like a chameleon according to where, with whom, and in which stage of life he happens to be. As a father, he behaves in a particular manner. As a husband, he takes up a different line of behavior. As a lover, he is yet another person again. As a friend, he has quite another attitude. As a "worker," he is a very different man altogether. He acts these "roles" unconsciously. They are all externalized social modes of his contradictory, fragmented self. We are supreme dissemblers, knowingly or unknowingly, and feign to be what we are not. Seldom are we our natural selves.

When a "picture" is in abeyance, we get a glimpse of the real person behind it. At odd moments, we peel off our "uniforms" and show ourselves as we truly are. In general, however, "pictures" and "roles" prevent us from any real understanding of ourselves as we internally are. Consider some of these "pictures:" "I'm a respectable man," "I'm of noble birth," "I'm a self-made man," "I'm a wronged man," "I'm brilliant," and that priceless burst of egoism, "Do you know who I am?" This has the stamp of man at his most egoistic moment, reckless and unbridled.

The less a man is, the more "airs" he is likely to put on, though he may be holding a very high position or status. It is yet another fallacy we embrace so fondly that a man who sits on a high and gilded chair must be "great."

We have our own attitudes in life. We see others through our "attitudes." We have a fixed way of "taking" other people, typical points of view and typical ways of regarding situations, events and things. "Attitudes" never think, but they connect us with various objects and make them important or unimportant as we look at them and how we regard them.

Consider the "attitude" of persons who occupy the highest offices in state or enjoy the most exalted status in society. They tend, with the rarest of exceptions, to identify themselves completely with the office or place which appears impregnable. This breeds in them an awful vanity, arrogance and exaggerated sense of their importance. They make themselves unapproachable. The "plus" of their position becomes a gaping "minus" in their internal life. *Sans* office and *sans* status—"*sans* everything," as Shakespeare ends his "Seven Ages of Man" monologue addressing this topic. Such conceited persons are reduced to a pitiable condition. With the halo gone, the health of the health of these persons begins to deteriorate fast, and they do not long survive the "neglect" and obscurity of their "fallen" state. They were once so full of demands, imperious and very jealous of their perks and privileges, "hop[ing] high up to ascend on fortune's wheel," and yet the wheel of fortune finally has brought them to their just desserts. (Sebastian Brandt, *The Ship of Fools*; Alexander Barclay, trans.)

We pay for every wrong attitude, for every lie to ourselves and to others, for every negative state, for hard unforgiving treatment of others and for aggressions and transgressions committed in our sheer intoxication of power and status.

A person believes he is choosing freedom for himself and celebrating his sense of self, not seeing that what he considers as "himself" is really a number of fixed attitudes, continually acting on him, without his even being aware of them. The last thing people will do is to think for themselves, for thinking is too difficult for most. They would rather go along with the attitudes they have already acquired and the mindset that goes with them. If people were to realize that they always say and do the same things, always take up the same "positions" and always maintain the same prejudices, they will then become aware that they have been "dead" persons. It is remarkable how psychologically "dead" persons seem to have a long life. We meet the living "dead" everywhere: walking in the streets, working in offices, shops and factories, enjoying themselves in clubs, cinemas and theatres and praying in temples, mosques and churches. This awful condition is not revealed until we begin to "see" it in ourselves.

We think we can take in new ideas any time we want. This is not possible, for the mind is already choked with fixed attitudes and prejudices. We nonetheless feel we have an open mind. In this darkness and ignorance of ourselves, we live and die ascribing to ourselves what we do not possess. We think we are consistent in our ideas and behavior, and when we express or do something contradictory, we fail to see any discrepancy. This is due to the action of certain buffers, which are the most terrible things in us. They are there to ease the shock of contradictions. If a man were to see and feel all the contradictions that are within him, he could not live and act as complacently as he lives and acts now. He would experience constant friction and unease. He must either destroy contradictions or cease to see or feel them. Yet with internal buffers, he ceases to see and feel them. He is surrounded by people who live, think, feel and speak like him, under the influence of buffers. The sudden removal of buffers, if that were at all possible, would drive him mad: he would lose all idea of himself. These buffers weaken and lose their hold when there is a heightening of awareness and consciousness.

To come to the right attitude is to come to a point of equilibrium between opposites. It is to walk with the right posture. A wrong attitude distorts our relationship with persons and to events. How little aware we may be of this! We may feel that others owe us right behavior, that we deserve better treatment, more appreciation and greater recognition. We often ask what others think of us, how they feel about us and what they say behind our back. As Robert Burns put it with wit as well as wisdom in his poem "To a Louse:":

> O wad [would] some Power the giftie gie
> [give] us
> To see oursel[ve]s as ithers [others] see us!
> It wad [would] frae [from] mony a blunder
> free us.
> An' foolish notion . . .

All feelings that others owe us and we owe them are not of deep psychological consequence to our inner development, for if we make many demands and requirements, we make life very difficult for ourselves. We show objection to this or to that. We make this or that demand before we feel satisfied or agree to anything. If we live by care for ourselves alone and regard ourselves as the axis around which all things must revolve, not only do we become shut in, we also destroy ourselves in the end. Ours is a thoughtless life, unmindful of the nature of things. Thoughtfulness or mindfulness has a different flavor. It lays a foundation for the right relationships to persons and objects. We should show proper consideration to the feelings and wishes of others, in spite of our awareness of their quirks and faults. Our inner attitude towards them will then rest on a firm, honest foundation. "There is no outward sign of courtesy that does not rest on a deep moral foundation," Goethe writes in his *Elective Affinities.* "The proper education would be that which communicated the sign and the foundation of it at the same time." (James Froude, trans.)

We do not see one another as we are or any object as it is. The outer world reaches us, as it were, through numerous distorted lenses. Habits of thought persist throughout life. We become conditioned to a set pattern of thinking and feeling and build "associations" accordingly. Truth for us is a habit of mind. We get upset when people do not think and behave as we expect. They fail to correspond to the "associations" and set ideas we have of them. This is conditioned living, which is unfree—cribbed, cabined and confined. Conditioned thinking leads to an extremely unimaginative and pedestrian view of life and the world. We judge others inflexibly without pity and without understanding. We do not have to live such a barren, insipid life, for if we could see within ourselves the very things which we judge in others, it would give rise to feelings of sympathy, mercy and forgiveness. No one can be "good" if he is not capable of doing "bad." He would be an emasculated creature, and his "goodness" is not really goodness at all. Catching at petty, mean little things will not broaden our minds nor give depth to our lives. We will remain ensconced in petty details, minor arguments and trivialities.

The mind of man contributes to its own enslavement by its conditioned thinking, habitual attitudes and borrowed beliefs and opinions. To create one's life, one has to rid oneself of these tendencies and cultivate mindfulness—to "distance" oneself from events and situations, whether involved inside or outside them, in order to develop a correct perspective and outlook towards others. Then would a man take that seriously which others treat lightly and treat that lightly which others take seriously.

CHAPTER 9

Emotions and Feelings

Our emotions, as we express them in daily life, show us in a very poor light. They are almost always negative, mean and paltry. If we were really aware of them, we would be shocked and horrified. We see people, events, situations and objects darkly and create for ourselves a darker world through these emotions and feelings. We indulge in self-pity and are conscious of injured self-love. We are full of resentment towards people, and in the secret of our hearts there lurks a gnawing feeling to "pay back" or "get even" with those who have not treated us well.

If we were attentive to our internal life, we would notice that in negative states there is always inner talking, which may find expression long after in outer talking. If we observe this monologue that goes on in a continuous stream within us, we would just find half-truths, or truths connected in the wrong way or with something added or omitted in the process. Even when we pay compliments, they are most often injected with an internal reservation, taking back with one hand what is given by the other. How negative we really are towards others!

Watch people in the streets when they are off guard. Notice their lips moving in silent talking and their faces showing tensions and pressures of their negative states. They are not conscious of the monologue, nor of the tense states which hold them as if in a vice. Only inner attention, which is put in motion by a state of awareness, can stop this inner talking and the negative states it gives rise to, acting and reacting on each other.

While this monologue is extremely harmful to our interior life, *a dialogue*, with ourselves, is very useful to our positive development. We become the observers and the observed at the same time and come to notice all the twists, tricks and feigning of our spurious feelings towards others. We are made aware of our evil states, and the shocks we suffer lead to a change in us.

A man can think differently more easily than he can feel differently. A thought does not affect us in the same way as an emotion does. Watch a person who is vexed. He may pretend there is nothing the matter with him, even forcing a smile in order to prove it. Yet within, he is all turbulence. An emotional crisis shakes us to our roots in a way no thought ever could. We are far more identified with our feelings than we are with our thoughts.

People love to say unpleasant and wretched things to one another. There is hardly any goodwill or charity in our ordinary state of emotions. To hate is easy, but to love is very hard. To hate to be negative is especially difficult. Negative states breed other negative states, and we go round and round in a vicious circle of these unpleasant feelings.

There is a tendency, very disquieting, in most of us to make a problem of anything that comes to our attention or for our consideration. Instead of making "crooked things straight" (Isaiah 42:16), we turn the straight and the simple into the crooked and the involved.

Worry and worrying can make any matter more harassing. Worry kills more people than accidents on roads. There are persons who "love" to worry, and they derive a perverted pleasure in worrying over trifles.

Suspicion drags down all human relations to the lowest plane as we read the worst motives into people. We have to realize our own tendency towards deceit and malice before we fall into these moods of suspicion and slander. Slandering, vilifying and distorting are all very damaging. They cause us to recoil in disquiet.

People show a tendency to become hostile and inimical to persons, ideas and things which they fail to comprehend. Whoever in history has introduced a new idea, a new way of doing things or a new approach to a vexing problem – whoever has founded a new religion, paved the way for a new style of life or broken customs and conventions—has always been hounded, persecuted and killed.

However unreasonable or immoral an action is, man has a compulsive urge to rationalize it. In his most depraved state, he still has an itch to find an excuse or justification for his heinous crimes. A strange madness darkens his understanding, and he persists in his contumacious ways.

We are completely engulfed in the multifarious situations of life and we make a pit of negativity, hopelessness and self-pity for ourselves. Self-pity itself is an inverted expression of a dark, subtle egoism within us. We can say a thousand hurtful things and poison others with our negative emotions and then feel quite pleased with ourselves, finding nothing wrong with turning the whole place into a hell.

Perhaps the most lethal negative emotions spring from feelings of injustice, resentment and indignation. What havoc they can wreak!

The events and situations of daily life build for us frustrations and we remain caught in a web of dark moods, our will paralyzed. We just allow ourselves to be dragged into things, or things drag us.

A negative person is quick to notice what we have neglected to say or do. His cognition is often deep and subtle. Suspicion, resentment and indignation make him abnormally sensitive to the "hidden" meanings of our words, our glances, our hesitations and even our intonations.

People gloat over the misfortune of others. They are prepared to believe all the lies and malicious things that gossip spreads about them.

Cruelty is a terrible fact of life—to inflict pain often becomes a sport with man. Some of the games he has invented to amuse himself reach the grossest or the most subtle stages of cruelty that can be imagined. Man was thrown to the beasts, and the gladiators were pitted to death against one another to amuse the ancient Romans. People take perverse pleasure inflicting injury on God's creatures, and of all living things except perhaps the praying mantis, man has always been the harshest and the most pitiless upon his own kind, often in a cold and calculated manner. Witness how slaves were treated throughout history everywhere. Even Aristotle, writing in his work *Politics,* considered slavery a natural thing and saw nothing wrong in it, even considering some human beings "slaves by nature" (Chapter V; William Ellis, trans.).

This is the darkest chapter of man in history: the way he caught slaves and worked them to death without a qualm of conscience! Nothing could be more revolting to man's inherent dignity as man than slavery, except his other tendency to degrade himself by worshipping all objects in nature instead of God, his Creator (for this makes us worship creatures in fear to ward off misfortune, sorrow, grief and misery).

The worst lot is the evil brood of hypocrites, the Tartuffes of this world. How "smooth" and "polished" is their exterior and how hideous their interior! They sow discord, dissension and strife as well as revel in creating chaos and confusion, and it is little wonder that the Italian Renaissance poet Dante assigns such sowers of discord to the nethermost circle of hell.

The most common failing of humans is "gossip" and next is unhealthy curiosity. Gossip may do harm to the character gossiped about but, far more, it destroys the confidence in the man who gossips. Mockery, back-biting and slander are just as odious as stabbing one's own friend in the back. Idle talk puts one to heavy "sleep."

It is startling what a change an emotion can affect. A moment of jealousy can hurl a man from wild happiness to the gloomiest mood. Envy, jealousy and spite play havoc with our lives. Doctors, lawyers, engineers, scientists, artists, writers, poets, theologians, scholars and technicians all get so coiled round these negative and obsessive feelings that they do not even make an attempt to get themselves, uncoiled from the crushing embrace of these crippling emotions. What a distinguished list of talent and genius! Yet, is there a more devastating commentary on the internal behavior of persons with other persons in allied professions?

There are others who can neither forgive nor forget. They have a deep-seated memory, a very negative characteristic which slowly destroys them.

When we are negative with a person, all the unpleasant, unsavory things which were apparently long forgotten come back to our consciousness, and we say nasty things and hurt them as much as we can.

The most awful thing that happens to a man who is very negative with another person is to put himself under his power, without his ever being aware of it. If a man hates another man, he puts himself entirely in his power, without ever realizing it.

The more we express negative emotions the more they feed on us. We are almost always negative with others, but merely pointing out to them their faults will produce negative results only. What irritates us in others is usually their mechanicalness. This is one source of negative states. Our reaction of irritation is just as mechanical, of which we may be blissfully unaware.

To be in the grip of negative emotions is to be under their bondage. The trouble is we actually enjoy different forms of slavery. People love their negative emotions, and if someone were to try to remove them, he would merely earn their hatred.

Man spends his energy mostly on unnecessary and unpleasant emotions, on the expectation of misfortunes, on bad moods, on haste and fantasies, and on being fretful and irritable.

We do not realize that negative emotions and feelings fill the atmosphere in which we live and breathe with a psychic disturbance. A profound disequilibrium affects every one of us. A negative state is inherently evil in intention. It may transgress all bounds of reason, descending towards more distortion, greater falsity, more ugliness, violence, cruelty, torture, murder and utter lack of redemption. The leer of Satan is here, standing with the jaws of hell open wide. All evil seeks to harm. The pity is we do not know how to do good or be good to others. It is all too easy to hurt. In a negative state, many self-injurious distortions are made and in this infernal tangle many remain most of their lives.

All negative emotions are unnecessary, and the power of negative states is baffling and shows how ignorant we are of what moves within us. The pull of what will drag us down to misery and hell cannot be explained if we take ourselves as a unity. This is one of our major illusions that prevent us from awakening.

Violence is the antithesis to understanding. The more negative a man is, the less he understands and the more violent he is apt to become. To react to violence is very easy, to understand is most difficult.

In violence, one man forces another man to act in the way the former desires, showing an utter lack of concern and indifference to the latter's person and life.

We are just as open to violence within as we are without. A small being which loves his own petty self and shuts out all others soon reaches a limit of tolerance and bursts into violence.

Xenophon gives the opinion of Socrates on "envy." He says, "Considering what envy was, he decided it to be certain uneasiness, not such, as arises however at the ill-success of friends, nor such as is felt at the good success of enemies, but those only, he said, were envious, who were annoyed at the good success of their friends." (John Selby Watson, trans.)

This thought is also posited in the writings attributed to King Solomon in the Old Testament and Jesus Sirach in the Deuterocanon (Apocrypha):

"Wrath is cruel and anger outrageous, but who is able to stand before envy?" (Proverbs 27:4)

"The envious man hath a wicked eye..." (Ecclesiasticus 14:8)

One of the most shocking things one finds in life, everywhere and in all conditions, is the pervasive habit of lying. People lie over matters which are trifles, and they lie over matters which are grave and serious, little realizing that this odious habit is at the center of many evils that plague human life.

It is simply not possible for a liar to grow and develop. Lying makes one false, for one deceives by telling lies. A habitual liar turns into a compulsive liar. His inner self is terribly ugly and distorted. He is so warped that he is the most despicable example of pretense. He exists in an extreme state of unreality, completely alienated from his true self. He has closed himself to all self-development. At the same time, he may be most brilliant.

How lightly people lie and pretend, putting on a thousand disguises! A mere gesture, a look, a sigh, an inflection, a heart-broken expression or an illness are a few of these disguises. The fact that people take lying and pretense so lightly go to indicate that they are smug and satisfied with themselves just as they are and are least interested in self-improvement. It would be a mockery to talk of self-evolution to them, its meaning and significance, as it would be like "speaking to a wall."

The eternal contention is always and ever between truth and falsehood. Those who lie and pretend are children of darkness, and our world is riddled with them.

Everyone has his own form of pride and vanity, and they seem quite natural to him. Pride can become part of the will, but vanity cannot ever be so. The density of pride is greater, and more can be done and more can be endured from pride. There is a pride that springs from a profound sense of human dignity and would pay any price to uphold it. Pride can turn into shame and humility in the presence of what is higher. A proud look is quite different from a vain look. When pride is turned outwards, it can be an accessory to vanity. If it is turned inwards, it may help the man in his work on himself. Vanity is always damaging, except perhaps in very small doses. We are permitted to ascribe to ourselves a little of any success and achievement that have come our way, but the trouble is we like to talk and boast about our successes. Even when we are silent, we are thinking about them.

Strange as it may seem, asceticism can transform into a dangerous sort of pride, destroying in the process the very spirit which was meant to be developed at the expense of the flesh. Self-abasement, too, is often an inverted, cold pride, subtly exploiting and undermining power and authority to gain its own purposes. The pride of false humility and the humility of genuine pride are the great paradoxes of life.

There are people who pride themselves on being proud, and there are others who say they have no pride, of which they are yet proud. The proud man will always quarrel with the proud, but he may agree on a common question of pride, such as pride of race or birth.

Pride can become an obstacle in any development of self. "Thus does the Lord set a seal over the heart of every proud and haughty one (man)." (Holy Qur'an; 40:35)

When we perceive and understand the cold, hard and unforgiving quality of pride, we come to realize how necessary it is to eliminate it in us. We also enable ourselves to see the state of those we condemn through it. Vanity likes to strut and craves for an audience, but it is not necessarily concerned with outward appearance. We always try to justify ourselves, even when we know better, for pride and vanity will not let us yield to others.

While a distinction can be made between pride and vanity, conceit and vanity are interchangeable. A conceited man is a vain man, and a vain man is a conceited man. A very vain person, like a liar, has closed himself to all self-development. Those who are vain and conceited have a gaping void in their interior lives.

Vanity desires to be placed first, like the two disciples of Jesus, who wanted to sit, one on his left and the other on his right hand, in heaven. Yet pride is rather in what Peter exclaimed to Jesus: "Though I should die with thee, yet will I not deny thee." (Matthew 26: 35) Nonetheless, Peter denied him.

A man who acts from a desire to make a good impression and gain the esteem of others has no inner goodwill. People attribute all sorts of fine qualities to themselves on the flimsiest of grounds, but they have not been tested.

A man may seem conceited and boastful on the surface and actually feel poor and inadequate within himself. The opposites are mixed in us in very strange ways.

The "happiness" that comes from being first, or having most, or looking best, is not genuine happiness. It depends, uneasily, on what others think of us or tell us and its effect is short-lived. It needs continual re-stimulation.

Where we are vain, there we are blind to ourselves. We refuse to see ourselves as we are. We may not appear vain and yet take ourselves very seriously. We wrap ourselves in our own seriousness, of which we are vain. Many of us are incapable of laughing at our own follies and *faux pas*, or else we may just pretend to laugh at our own selves.

A person who is very vain cannot make any contact with anything genuine, even though he may wish to do so. His own posturing and pretense would render him incapable of evolving into a conscious man.

We harbor within many illusions about life and the world, and yet the paradox is we firmly believe we have no illusions. It is others who have them. All illusions are lies and deceptions. We run after appearances and chase shadows.

How difficult it is to catch even a glimpse of self-idolatry and all its spurious creations. It contracts everything, puts on many disguises and lives on flattery and constant attention. It craves to be admired while it feigns to be modest.

Self-idolatry is at heart callous. It cannot tolerate being ridiculed. Nothing it does is ever disinterested, without motive and purpose. Its constant desire is to increase its own self-merit. If there are charitable endowments, the real object is to enhance the donor's name. What the motive is and what it is presented to be are not quite the same. Even anxious concern for others is really to show oneself in the best light, for the heart remains cold and insensitive.

Where there is a strong sense of "me," "my" and "mine," man is at his most egotistical, being very self-centered, possessive and demanding – in effect, incapable of "letting go" of attention, things and objects. The "me," "my" and "mine" focus all the attention, inner and outer, on oneself alone. The rest is peripheral and counts just to the extent it listens, humors and pampers.

Convention and the false social values we live by build an acquired conscience in us and make it very difficult for us to become real persons. There is a mixture of self-love, imitation and fear in the acquired conscience. It is turned outwards towards what others think of our conduct and behavior. There is a compulsive urge to conform to the patterns set by society, lest one be "ostracized." As Joshua Loth Liebmann observes, "By infinitely multiplying this neccessity to conform, at the expense of of developing the unique, individual 'self,' society succeeds in [...] instill[ing] in [man] a pattern which is so rigid that he is often unable to express his true self at all." Conventional life is plagued by a deep unease and anxiety. The social pressures and traditional ways rob man of his inherent right to freedom to shape his life in his own way without fear and without pressure. The most unimaginative life is the "conformed' life, lived under social conventions and their psychological pressures. It is also the most "unfree."

A man may appear most holy and yet have the basest interior psychologically. We seem to forget that the devil has the face of an angel. A man may wallow in self-righteousness even when he is in the thick of an atrocious act in the name of his faith and belief. The ways God is invoked by man to justify his acts, however odious their nature, would freeze the warm blood coursing through the arteries.

A man may do good, speak the truth, behave justly, all for the sake of reputation, appearances, honor or gain—yet in himself *will* nothing good and think nothing of truth. The more a man is turned in *upon* himself, the less real he is *in* himself.

The first step towards self-evolution is the love of *uses*. Anyone who has the simplicity to take real pleasure in whatever he does and enjoys and appreciates the ordinary, simple things of life begins to move away from egoism. He is on the way to an authentic life.

There is pure sensuality, the sensuality of the Song of Songs. Nature's mysterious and awesome ways, her infinite variety and creativity, her ineffable beauty, magnificence and grandeur restore us to vigor and freshness, to joy and delight in life. We then come under the spell of Eros and the creative spirit awakens in us.

There is impure sensuality, which drags us down to ugliness, grossness and vulgarity, ending in negation and death of the spirit. We are cast under the malignant power of Thanatos, the ancient Greek manifestation of death.

There is pure sympathy, unstinted, welling up from an understanding heart, and there is sympathy calculated, expecting something in return.

Pure and impure emotions differ very little in their outer manifestations. Pure emotions are always objective in nature. They apprehend the value and significance of real things.

Impure emotions are unreal, illusory, irrational and subjective. All sentimental feelings are of this nature. Any pretense about our emotions ends in self-deception, a dangerous state of the soul. When a man succeeds in freeing himself from impure emotions he arrives at a correct understanding of himself and the world. All impure emotions are like concave and convex mirrors, ever distorting the image of the self and of the world.

Some emotions close us, yet others open us. Pure emotions reveal to us new and surprising facets of objects and impart a marvelous glow to our understanding. It is impossible to reach a correct understanding of the nature of things through impure emotions.

Some find it difficult to understand the difference between a thought and a feeling, others between a feeling and a sensation, still others between a thought and a passing impulse.

We often behave very differently from what we feel. This shows how false and dishonest we are with our own selves and with others.

All emotions are useful in their proper expression. They are akin to an extra sense disclosing to us the states of man and the nature of things. Yet impelled and driven by impure emotions, we cannot use them except to create further illusions. If we could use them to apprehend objects as they are, we would obtain new insights and understanding of the Cosmos.

Relaxation is essential after intense activity. Truly relaxed, we give ourselves an opportunity to see, observe, think and evaluate without hurry and without tension. Hurried movements induce hurried and anxious thoughts and feelings. We must study "posture." Certain postures lead to certain thoughts and feelings. Correct posture is therefore important. This is a matter of proper training of our physical movements. A trained athlete is a man who knows how to eliminate unnecessary movements. To train oneself is to learn how not to do things which are unnecessary.

CHAPTER 10

Words, Ideas and Prayer

"Words are the shadow of reality." – Rumi
"Our greatest difficulty is, that language is
not adequate to express our ideas; because
our words refer to *things*, and are images
of what is substantial and material."

–Albert Pike, *Morals and Dogma*
(Chapter 26)

Words mean many things. They convey meanings, and the insight of meanings depends on who uses them and how he makes use of them. If words are used merely as words without real ideas behind them they will only produce a babble of confusion. Slogans and clichés of "associative thinking" will fill the air.

There is a discussion as to whether or not words are arbitrary in the Platonic dialogue *Cratylus*, in which it is argued that the names of things – words – "are natural... and there is a truth or correctness in them." (B. Jowett, trans.) Regrettably, there are trends in modern philosophy and linguistics which negate this insight in favor of the view that words (and indeed language itself) are arbitrary and without fixed meaning.

Yet it is true that man talks too much, and he writes too much. If all the trillions of words he speaks and spouts were to be placed as "solid objects" in space, then no room whatsoever would be left for any other thing or object there. His speech and his writing are most often verbiage. Imagine the chaos and confusion that this verbiage inflicts upon man. He is swamped with words. Confounded and harassed man is not one whit wiser than before. Verbiage disguises an empty head or hides the poverty of ideas behind a facade of learning.

Words have their own emotional and psychological background, revealing a man's likes and preferences as well as his distastes and prejudices.

No two persons may mean and understand the same thing by the same word. This is at the root of the misinterpretations of the teachings of sages, prophets and philosophers. The creators of great works of literature and the founders of the great faiths of mankind were followed by their interpreters: at first the disciples, later disciples of the disciples and then a long line of critics, all giving their own versions and interpretations of the words and the works of the Masters. There have been wars of words and wars to kill in order to impose particular interpretations. When a word breaks loose from its right connection of ideas, it becomes dangerous, a source of diabolical mischief, in the hands of every uneducated or unprincipled man. In this sense, the "learned" are more devilish than the others.

We can have richer or poorer ideas behind the words we use, according to the level of our intelligence and understanding. The density of meaning of a word depends upon the quality and level of ideas behind it. A word is nothing by itself. Its significance is due to the inflow of meaning it releases. Ideas exist by themselves and if they are not properly handled confusion and bitter strife take hold of the affairs of life. The literal and logical approach can destroy ideas and lead to very dangerous consequences.

"Double-think," as George Orwell called it in his dystopian novel *Nineteen Eighty-Four*, is a contortion of words which mean anything the user would want them to mean. They then become murderous in intent and purpose. The most conspicuous users are those who have established and who run "closed systems" of totalitarian states.

Words have a mystic power over things. There is the strange potency ascribed to incantations, interdictions and curses. They express something far beyond the moment. They bind man to things that are contingent and produce psychological states that cast a spell upon him.

Some ideas penetrate to the soul and leave their mark for life. It is quite possible that a wrong trace may be left. A man can catch an idea in many different ways: as a thinker, as a poet, as a writer, as an artist, as an architect, as an engineer, or as a scientist. If a man is earnest to evolve, he must prepare himself for the reception of higher ideas opening on to deeper levels of reality.

The words a man speaks conceal more than they reveal his thoughts and inward impulses. There is a world of difference between words and *realization*. Realization is like a beam of light which, like a laser, penetrates to the inmost depth of a matter, an issue, or a situation.

A man may know many fine and beautiful words, speak effortlessly and fluently and yet be very far from any inner growth and understanding. The situations of life have many hidden traps, traps which will catch many unwary persons.

Words may in fact stand in the way of understanding. Man does not experience the world as it is. He sees it through a fog of words. He cerebrates through words and rarely, if ever, intuits. He has a tendency to escape into theories, for he finds them safe. They also satisfy his passion for intellectual acrobatics.

Ideas become distorted when people begin to invent their own theories and explanations for them. The deepest and the profoundest are beyond words. The language of man cannot express or catch the subtlest nuances of thought and feeling, for it is an instrument of the outward life of solids. The experiences of the inward life of man dwell in the intangibles of the spirit and the mind and, far more, of higher states of consciousness, a vast, mysterious field of psychic activity, which it is not possible for human language to express.

Our minds cannot formulate even things of our outward experience in the right way as they truly are. We can try to express them as near to truth and reality as our feeble understanding will allow.

There is a common feeling that "writing" is not difficult, if only one sat behind a desk and pushed his pen. Yet this is a fallacy. The moment one takes up a pen to formulate one's ideas expression of them, as one desires, eludes one. What appears on paper is at best a poor approximation to the subtle movements of the mind and the spirit. Only that writing has profound influence which is written with one's own blood.

Prayer may be in words or in an attitude of reverence. They are worlds apart. Prayer is man's effort to seek release from the mechanical state, which is the normal state of man in outward life.

In Rumi›s Discourse # 38, he presents a parable in which the Prophet Muhammad (peace be upon him) says: "There is no prayer without the heart." The heart is the seat and source of inspiration, and intuitive understanding.

The Prophet Jesus saw the Pharisees and said:

> And when thou prayest, thou shalt not
> be as the hypocrites are: for they love to
> pray standing in the synagogues and in
> the corners of the streets, that they may
> be seen of men. Verily I say unto you, they
> have their reward. (Matthew 6: 5)

When a man supplicates himself before God in his ordinary state to have his wish granted, whatever it may be, little does he realize that he may be unfit to receive what he prays to be given or it may do him harm if it were given to him. Nothing can happen, for in this so-called "waking" state, the man is neither conscious of himself nor conscious of the nature of things. He has first to pass from the state of ignorance and darkness to the state of "light" and full awareness. If a man works neither on the line of knowledge nor on the line of being and yet prays for wisdom, his view of the Universe is very naïve. He must realize the harshness of things and the price that has to be paid. He has first to get rid of childish and sentimental notions, "to put away childish things." (1 Corinthians 13: 11) When being and knowledge are fused, understanding comes, and when understanding comes, wisdom comes.

All prayer invoked in self-pity is worthless.

Prayer for others is possible only through understanding their troubles, yet a man understands others in so far as he understands himself. Insight into their true condition will help him to pray in the right spirit.

To pray when a man should be making his own effort is prayer wasted. "For whatsoever a man soweth, that shall he also reap." (Galatians 6: 7) No prayer can alter the operation of this law.

A man has to be extremely careful in his prayer, lest it interfere in any way with the freedom or affect the well-being of another person.

That prayer alone is truly an inner reality when the whole man prays in a conscious state. Then there is presence of the heart, right understanding and detachment from worldly concerns and above all a profound sense of one's "creatureliness" before God, allowing for communion in awe.

To sit and meditate on a particular theme creates, unconsciously, an inner conflict, for the act is divorced from the rest of one's daily conduct of life. There is an artificial break, a detached fragment out of tune with the tenor of one's life, which is shot through with lies and dishonesty.

The harmony and rhythm must come from the activity of life itself, in facing reality in an honest and positive manner, without evasion and without self-deception. There is a state of inner awareness. Meditation is never apart from life; it is an integral part of life itself. The dynamic stillness in the midst of activity is meditation.

To realize its meaning ponder over the words: "*Be still* and know that I am God." (Psalm 46: 10; italics by the author) God dwells in the center of man's being.

An ordinary man, who is mechanical in most things most of the time, will ask, "How is it possible to be still in the thick of activity?" In our ordinary state, when things "ride" on us, and we are vexed with problems, we would be "noisy" and "agitated" inside and could never dream of stillness. For us, meditation would be meaningless. Our prayers, when we pray, are mechanical. They fail to touch the ground of our being. We are literally Pharisees.

There are, however, persons who look just as ordinary as we are, and yet their interior life is dynamic and creative. In the storm and stress of life, they are fully capable of withdrawing to the stillness of their being. Their sight is deep and clear. Their approach to their work is correct and their attitude is right. They therefore perform their task truly and well. The dynamic stillness that they consciously realize within themselves comes to them effortlessly due to the elevation of their emotions and the profound awareness and understanding of their "being" to the nature, quality and level of things and objects in the world.

This is the best form of meditation, the spiritual exercise that is never divorced from the dust and noise of the world.

CHAPTER 11

Boredom

"Idleness is the burial of a living man. For an idle person is so useless to any purposes of God and man, that he is like one who is dead, unconcerned in the changes and necessities of the world; and he only lives to spend his time, and eat the fruits of the earth."

- Albert Pike, *Morals and Dogma*
(Chapter 5)

The most ancient disease of man is "boredom." Idleness has bored him. Work has bored him. Pleasure, when it reaches the point of satiation, has bored him. He must ever look for fresh titillation to escape boredom. He has thus swung between desire and fulfillment and back from fulfillment to desire throughout his history.

When we are fed-up, sated with food and sex, or when we drift, we increase psychological entropy, which is the same as psychological "sleep." Everyone has experienced at some time or other a feeling of heaviness, of emptiness which so easily takes hold of us with the thought of the sameness of existence, the soulless routine in which we are trapped. The days stretch endlessly, living the same life and doing the same things. This violates something deep in us that should be free from the subservience of the senses, except to the degree that it is necessary.

The more conscious we are, the less we shall be bored. We should not let one day run into another, making a blur, in which awareness of ourselves is very slight. If we were more conscious, we would not do what we do and think and feel as we do. Only a naïve mind can believe that the passage of time in and of itself means progress. Time is not progress, and length of time is nothing in itself.

To move away from feelings of boredom, a man must first awaken himself from the "sleep" of mechanical life. The keenness and tang to life come when we move away from mechanical life to creative life. The personal self makes an inward journey to greater integrity, purity of vision, and wholeness. We begin to reach higher levels of the conscious life.

Life is a bad proposition for man in the mechanical state. Its difficulties fall on all alike, but in different ways. There is no escape from its lash until we leave behind the mechanical state. We then become equal to life.

It is very difficult to draw a boundary between life, with all its multifarious activities, and ourselves. The world is, after all, continually impinging on us all the time and we see jealousy, avarice, malice, hypocrisy, cruelty, pride, vanity, resentment, indignation and many other negative emotions making life around us unpleasant and disagreeable. Is it ever possible for the human situation to improve if people remain what they are?

Would it not be marvelous if we began to "unknow" and became a little quieter and moved towards the real "I," which is reached by the actual separation of the false from the real? Our life is lived on such a superficial plane that reality is obscured from us and what we take to be real is a mere travesty of it. Of what use is all the knowledge a man acquires when he is ignorant of himself, of who or what he is and of the real nature of things? "The curse of ignorance is that man without being good or wise is nevertheless satisfied with himself: he has no desire for that of which he feels no want." Thus states Socrates in the Platonic dialogue *Symposium* (Benjamin Jowett, trans.) and "the bubble reputation." (Shakespeare, "The Seven Ages of Man," As You Like It).

Many are the ways in which a man catches his own self in the snare made by his very hand. This snare is psychological, and he is the least aware of it when he is caught in it. The snare may come in the form of self-pity, resentment, envy, jealousy, lust or avarice or the desire to get even with the world for having been treated badly. It may come through deprivation, surfeit of things, drugs, liquor, smoking, gambling or some foolish escapade to escape boredom. These psychological traps lead to many physical ailments, which in the end prove fatal. Death is, of course, inescapable for all organisms, but most harrowing is the terrible suffering, the disabilities and the utter helplessness to which man is finally reduced. "Any man's death diminishes me," as the Metaphysical poet John Donne writes, "because I am involved in mankind." Yet much of this pain and suffering accumulate according to the way we live and how the world deals with us in our reckless drive to run away from the profound sense of insecurity that is inseparable from living in the world. If only we led a less mechanical life, if only we were a little more aware and conscious of the "price" we are made to pay for the thoughtless manner in which we squander the gift of life in the pursuit of phantasies and chimeras.

There are two kinds of suffering. One is fraudulent and the other real. Boredom is a fraudulent suffering, or to regard ourselves as worthy of special attention and consideration and feeling and to take umbrage that we have been neglected and ignored. Our self-esteem is terribly hurt. We brood and suffer, not realizing that we have caught ourselves in the noose of fraudulent suffering. The other kind of suffering is real, when we are fully conscious of the origin and nature of our suffering and the consequences which wait for us if we do not make the utmost effort to transcend ourselves from the lower to the higher. Fraudulent suffering closes us to higher levels of conscious life, while real suffering opens for us the way to higher development of our personal selves.

The overcoming of the past is one great line of personal work. Most people have such a store of unhappy memories which they have clung to with such tenacity that they find it very difficult to escape from these pathetic states, which only lead to negative emotions and "fraudulent" suffering. If a man were to look into his past searchingly, he would be shocked to discover that his life has been a mere imitation, impelled by urges and drives which are frantic efforts to keep up with the "Joneses" that there was really nothing genuine and sincere in that life. There was no integrity, no search for the meaning of things, no desire to understand the silent and subtle rebukes of the spirit moving in the depths of his being. There were too many weak spots, evasions, lies, hypocrisies and much dishonesty which have insidiously lodged themselves is his interior life.

He has to force them out to the surface that he may confront them, struggle and rid himself of their damaging effects for good. The whole of the past must be cancelled eventually. There must be nothing against anyone. We must cancel all of our debts, and since we are indebted to everyone we have ever known, whether in a positive or negative sense, in one way or another, it means that we have to put every relationship right. We must try to avoid both regret and blame, for they lead us nowhere. There is much to be learned from what may seem to be a lost opportunity. Whether it was lost or not depends not upon what we did in the past, but on how much understanding we can extract from it now. Our failings and mistakes give us far more understanding than what we consider as our virtues and successes, for, in a sense, these really make us blind and put us in darkness.

There is an old Stoic saying associated with Zeno and Chrysippus that we are tied to life "as a dog is tied to a cart." He has to run on with the cart if he does not want to be dragged by it. If we go to a thing from our own selves, our approach is positive. If we are dragged to it, then it becomes negative.

It is much too easy to "give up" and be resigned. Man is inherently lazy. We read in the *Odyssey* of Odysseus visiting "the land of Lotus and the flowery coast" where the lotus-eater inhabitants are described by Homer thus:

> They eat, they drink, and nature gives the
> feast

The trees around them all their food
produce:
[...] Nor other home, nor other care
intends,
But quits his house, his country, and his
friends.

(Homer, *Odyssey*, Book IX; Alexander
Pope, trans.)

As in Homer, man will always slide back into the state of
the lotus-eater if there was not something to goad him on.
He should never have more than a brief respite from his
labors, the task of working-out his destiny by developing
all his inner resources. There is inevitable struggle, travail
and—above all—the nagging sense of responsibility. How
else can he liberate himself from ignorance, illusions,
delusions, and negations?

The root of "angst." the basic anguish of being alive,
is in a way the Buddhist *dukkha*. This notion comes
up in the Western philosophy as well, suggested by
Schopenhauer and the twentieth-century existentialists.
This is the second kind of suffering. While more real and
more sincere than the fraudulent suffering of boredom or
ennui, it is man living without the full awareness of the
manifold possibilities of life.

CHAPTER 12

The Gift of Memory

Our memory is intimately related to our level of being. Indeed, our level of being is concomitant with our memory. Our present memory may be false or distorted, and we actually remember very little. It is doubtful we are able to remember anything accurately as it actually was or occurred in reality. Memory relies on our power of reception, and this is by no means objective. We may, for all we know, be inventing in trying to recall some past event or situation. Our imagination may be little more than fabrication. In this sense, our memories are lies. We cherish our memories, especially of things and events and situations which were, when we recall, happy and pleasant. Yet we seem to forget that our memories play many tricks on us. We experience so much, only to forget it all afterwards. So many things evaporate, even those we thought were so "important" that they were engraved our mind. Not a trace of many such memories may eventually be left. The reason, most prime for us, is that our past lives were lived in a general state of unawareness. We probably had very rare moments of living on a conscious level. What happened in those moments is indelibly recorded in the recesses of our being. The rest has been erased and remains as the fabrication of our supposed memory.

If it were ever possible to recall sensations which were exquisitely pleasurable, we would hate to move away from them. Yet how thin and pallid they do appear in recollection! Evanescence is all. Pleasurable sensations are savored to the full, but how soon they vanish and are no more! Man can never catch hold of the passing moment, however hauntingly lovely and fragrant it may be and make it his own as a permanent possession, to linger over it, to savor it to the full. No sooner does he stretch out his hand to catch it, it slips away from him, and he is left empty-handed and disconsolate, ever wistful to make his own that which can never be his, no matter what he has done. This is the universal order of things, and man is helpless in the face of such cosmic laws.

We occasionally have inner intimations and perceptions of the remembrance of things past, indicating a state higher than our common level. The traces of these past memories throw light on the inherent potential in man to evolve to higher levels of consciousness. We carry within us the seeds of growth to a higher conscious life. The most vivid and acute memory is never sought consciously. It comes at its own bidding in flashes or passive receptivity, when one's "personality" is quiescent. This is the recall of perceptions experienced, however briefly, in a state of what we may term "light."

We are able to act only because, of all living creatures, we alone have a memory, which has gathered together all the thoughts, emotions and acts of our past into the unity of our present life. We are therefore, in a profound sense, the result of our total memory. We maintain within us the organic and psychological effects of all the experiences, events and situations of our past. There is a memory behind our personal memory to which we rarely have an access, if at all, at the ordinary level of consciousness. Here everything has been recorded—everything we have said, done, seen and experienced. This is man's real *memory*, and—mercifully for us—it is concealed from us. In moments of higher conscious states, the door to this memory is opened to us, but only to the extent we can stand it, without losing our mind. We have buffers that prevent us from becoming conscious in real, most interior memory. This is the Book of Life which is opened at death, and we shall be judged by ourselves. "What have you done with your life that is sufficient?" we will be asked. Under the immutable order of things, "Justice" stands for an upright life, but this leaves no accounts behind at death.

The great Swedish mystic Emanuel Swedenborg once wrote:

> The interior memory is such that there are inscribed in it all the particular things which man has at any time thought, spoken and done from his earliest infancy to extreme old age. Man has with him the memory of all these things, when he comes to another life; and is successively brought into all recollection of them.
>
> His past life may be shown to him in a vision. He remembers every detail of it and there is no possibility of his lying and concealing anything.
>
> - *The Heavenly Arcana* (No. 2474, "Genesis")

Swedenborg describes too the "light of the Lord" which permeates the hereafter, a light of ineffable brightness, which he himself glimpsed. This is the light of truth and understanding.

Chinese and Tibetan Buddhist literature abounds with accounts of those who glimpse the afterlife only to come back bodily into this world, as in Pu Songling's account of the dying "Buddhist Priest of Ch'ang-ch'ing:"

> [t]hey found he was already gone. The old priest was himself unconscious of death, and his soul flew away to the borders of the province of Honan [Henan] [...] Now it chanced that the scion of an old family residing in Honan [Henan], had gone out that very day [hunting] and was killed. Just at that moment the soul of the priest came by and entered into the body, which thereupon gradually recovered consciousness.
>
> (*Strange Stories from a Chinese Studio*; Herbert A. Giles, trans.)

The scholar Juan-Sebastián Gómez-Jeria has analyzed another Pu Songling "strange story" of one Dr. Tang, whose spirit transcends his body after uring a serious illness in which he awaits a review of the record of his life by King Wen Yang and the sage Confucius. Tang is eventually returned to the world of the living after a "death" of seven days. Gómez-Jeria notes that this review of one's life is a commonplace of what we today call the "near-death experience." We see this expressed in Tibetan Buddhist tradition as well.

In Bardo Thodol (a Buddhist work which has become known popularly as the Tibetan Book of the Dead), a dying or "clinically dead" person having a "near-death experience" senses his mind or soul depart from the body and finds himself in an alternate reality of *void*. He experiences disturbing whirring and whistling sounds, as if in a violent storm. In his "out-of-body experience," mourners who have been close to him in life are seen and heard, but they no longer perceive the "deceased" as a living person, despite his efforts to call out to them. He sees and hears his relatives and friends preparing the funeral as an invisible onlooker. It is as if he is in a body of light, but not a body in the earthly sense. He can penetrate physical objects, and "walls and so on are no obstacle [...] yielding to him as he pass[es]," to quote what we read of the Taoist priest with special powers at Lao-shan in yet another tale in *Strange Stories from a Chinese Studio*. The clinically dead people can transverse large spatial distances within a moment, often encountering a bluish light. One should advance towards this luminance with trust, faith and a humble spirit, the Tibetan Book of the Dead enjoins, and thus will result peace and satisfaction of the life well-lived, a reflection – a mirror, as it were—of all acts in life by which the deceased may be judged – again, a review of one's life as a whole. The Tibetans showed a degree of psychological insight and extra-sensory perception that was astonishing for a people whose "Buddhist" faith was riddled with indigenous, polytheistic practices.

The Holy Qur'an says: "And every man's fate have we fastened about his neck and on the Day of Resurrection will we bring forthwith to him a book, which shall be proffered to him wide-open. Read thy book: there needeth, none but thyself, to make an account against thee this day." (Holy Qur'an 17: 13-14).

God has given man life, and He alone can take it back when and in what manner it is His Will to do so. Those who take their own lives go against the Will of God and damn themselves as rebels against Him, their creator, no matter what pain and agony man may have to endure he has to treat his life as a trust from Him and to live it through and when the final moment comes to part from it, he willing or not, showing life and death belonged to Him, and he himself could exercise no will of his own.

Most of our memory of the past, memory of other people, of events and situations, and above all of our own selves, is mainly imagination. It is replete with personal emotions, which have to be pressed out until we begin to get flashes of higher conscious experience. We then arrive at a new kind of memory. This is like a clear mirror, without any blemish. Objective consciousness is attained when the memory is wiped clean of all subjective elements and not a trace of them is left.

When we go back into our past, we should try not to recall persons who have influenced us, for good or bad, but make an effort to see what we were like at different periods of our life. The psychological observation travels backwards slowly, step by step, stage by stage into the past. It is as if one took a train, put in the reverse gear, and it ran back through the same landscape, reviving the scenes as they were repassed, and we took mental notes of them, reconstructing our original impressions of them. It may, however, happen that we experience a sudden flash of consciousness extending way back into the past of what we have just begun to realize about ourselves now in the present moment. A sudden revelation of this nature will not come without a great deal of preparation. This experience is not at all pleasant, but how can we expect to reach a higher level of conscious experience if we are not prepared to endure it? We resent criticism and get upset and offended at the least thing that touches our self-esteem or conceit. Yet is this not the crux of the whole problem of the change of being, to "rise on stepping-stones/ Of [our] dead selves to higher things?" (Tennyson, "In Memoriam")

CHAPTER 13

Cause and Effect, End and Means

"You admire this tower of granite, weathering the hurts of so many ages. Yet a little waving hand built this huge wall, and that which builds is better than that which is built. The hand that built can topple it down much faster. Better than the hand, and nimbler, was the invisible thought which wrought through it; and thus ever, behind the coarse effect, is a fine cause, which, being narrowly seen, is itself the effect of a finer cause. Everything looks permanent until its secret is known. A rich estate appears to women a firm and lasting fact; to a merchant, one easily created out of any materials, and easily lost. An orchard, good tillage, good grounds, seem a fixture, like a gold mine, or a river, to a citizen; but to a large farmer, not much more fixed than the state of the crop. Nature looks provokingly stable and secular, but it has a cause like all the rest . . . Permanence is a word of degrees.

--Ralph Waldo Emerson, "Circles"

It is a grave fallacy to imagine that a good and desirable end can be reached regardless of the means used, that "the ends justify the means," as the political philosopher Machiavelli would have it in his work *The Prince*. The natural order of things imposes a condition which man ignores at his own peril, especially in the pursuit of raw power. It is an immutable rule that only good means will lead to a good end and bad and corrupt means to a vicious end. When we are not scrupulous about the means we employ to attain the end we pursue, then, inevitably, we shall vitiate all our acts and the end which we shall finally reach will take on the evil nature of our means. We must not forget that means and ends flow into each other. The end takes on the color of the means. As Emerson reminds us in his essay "Circles," "Cause and effect are two sides of one fact."

The whole of history is a battleground of ends and means. Rulers and conquerors have been least concerned about using the right means to realize the end they sought. Devious, deceitful and frightful means have led to devious, deceitful and frightful, ends and no wonder history is a record of horrible crimes committed by despots and tyrants in the name of God, religion and the welfare of humankind. Most individuals have shown very little regard for the right means to reach the end they have sought and desired. Not one of them has escaped the punishment which finally descended on them, to a man, in a thousand forms, of which they had not the remotest idea.

He who breaks the natural order of things, as it applies to the life of man, has to pay the price for it, the consequences that flow from human actions, unchanging, unchangeable, quietly and silently working, without haste and without rest, to the conclusions decreed, relentless, sure and certain. If only man lived a more conscious life, if only he cared for the right means to achieve the right end!

Every cause gives rise to an effect, and—as soon as the effect shows itself—it becomes a new cause in its turn, so that other effects may come into being. Causes thus go far back in time to their remotest origin. Yet it requires a very lucid and discerning mind to see the links of the flux of cause and effect, though they are not clearly discernable.

A materialist has only a limited conception of origins and causation, for he is not capable of seeing them beyond two dimensions.

The world is woven of freedom and necessity. If the law of causation operates, so does the law of indeterminacy and probability, under which particles behave, apparently, in an unpredictable manner. At the heart of Nature there is an impenetrable mystery. Chance and certainty, regularity and fluctuation, cause and effect, symmetry and dissymmetry are all parts of a complex pattern that weaves the Cosmic tapestry.

At every moment of time, everything is where it is and must be. Let one's consciousness expand so that it may read the meaning of it.

End, cause and effect form a triad. The effect could not exist without the cause, and the cause could not come into being without the end. The end is the cause of the cause, and it is so of the effect.

It is one thing to think *from* cause, another to think *of* cause, one thing to think *from* effect, another to think *of* effect and, to conclude the whole matter, it is one thing to think *from* end, another to think *of* end.

Every end is in every particular, and every particular is in the universal. They interpenetrate one another, and yet every particular is different and the universal is one and the same.

To see the Universe in a single leaf, or "To see the World in a grain of sand," as William Blake phrases it in his poem "Auguries of Innocence," is to become conscious of ends. One thing becomes myriad.

It is vital to understand that "something" is finite and that "nothing" is infinite. The infinite is itself not finite, which is to say we come to "nothing." We meet nothing but "nothingness." Reason loses its foothold here and falls into the Void. What then is the Universe?

Nothing happens in a man without a cause from the "unmanifest" world, but we do not see this. The "unmanifest" thought, for example, is the cause of the manifest action.

> Shallow men believe in luck, believe in circumstances: It was somebody's name, or he happened to be there at the time, or, it was so then, and another day it would have been otherwise. Strong men believe in cause and effect ("Essay on Worship")

CHAPTER 14

The Law of Polarity

"And of everything we have created pairs, that ye may receive instruction." (Holy Qur'an, 51: 49)

We would have inward peace,
Yet will not look within;
We would have misery cease,
Yet will not cease from sin;
We want all pleasant ends, but will use no harsh means;
We do not what we ought,
What we ought not, we do,
And lean upon the thought
That chance will bring us through;
But we are all the same—the fools of our own woes!
But our own acts, for good or ill, are mightier powers.

- Matthew Arnold, *Empedocles on Etna*
(Act I, Scene ii, lines 233-243)

All objects, wherever they are, lie hidden in their opposites. To everything there is an opposite, through which it exists and by which it is opposed.

Philo of Alexandria says, "That which is made up of both the opposites is one, and when this one is dissected, the opposites are brought to light."

It is said in the Book of Ecclesiasticus (42: 24) in the Deuterocanon (Apocrypha), "All things are double one against another…"

The opposites are connected like the two sides of a coin. Man is impelled by his desires. What meaning has self-control if he has no lust or desire? The Buddha taught that the root of evil was desire and hence man should rid himself of all desires if he wanted to attain Nirvana, whereas the teaching of Islam is the *refinement* of desire and not its elimination. To kill desire is to cancel the law of opposites, which is in operation in the Universe which man knows. Islam, therefore, conforms to this eternal order of things. Indeed, to conform to the eternal order of things is to be a Muslim.

Rumi, the thirteenth-century Persian poet and Sufi mystic, observed most acutely:

> So all things, though appearing opposite
> in relation to their opposites, in relation
> to the wise man are performing the same
> work and are not opposed. Show me the
> evil thing in this world wherein no good
> is contained and the good thing wherein
> no evil is contained. So evil and good are
> indivisible […] for good does not exist
> apart from evil. (A.J Arberry, trans.)

Good and evil are associated in a design or mosaic we call the world and without which no world could be. Black and white seem opposites while in reality they are two ends of shades of grey, their negative and positive limits. The lighter the shade, the nearer it is to white and the nearer it is to *light;* the darker the shade, the nearer it is to black and the nearer it is to *darkness.* What appears "good" may in effect not be "good" and what appears "bad" may in effect not be "bad." Good may be bad and bad may be good, for the universe has an astonishing display of opposites in operation. There is no man so bad that he does not have a redeeming quality in him, and there is no man so good that he does not have some tendency that may push him over the brink, for our view is partial, colored, and distorted. We see appearances and not the things as they really are. Behind these appearances lie hidden other meanings and realities.

The Law of Polarity is the Chinese Taoist Principle of *yin* and *yang* and instructs us on the nature of things as they operate in the Universe known to man. The great poet of the Arabic language Al-Mutannabi, in his *Divan,* wrote the dazzling line: "Things are made clear by their opposites."

It is through the interaction, the pull and play of polar opposites that the world moves and has its being. "Becoming" is the birth of duality. From duality spring the forces of action and reaction, attraction and repulsion, light and darkness, life and death. Growth proceeds by the spiral process of strife and contention, adjustment and right placement. The polarities in themselves are neither good nor bad. They are neutral and promote God's work in the phenomenal world of space and time. Whatever appears as chaos, anarchy, pain and suffering—the out-working of the Divine—would be seen as wholly *good* if viewed from the center of the Cosmic Whole.

The dark accentuates the light and good and evil appear as polar aspects of this Whole, perceived by man, as if "through a glass, darkly." (1 Corinthians 13: 12) The contraries, the antinomies, constitute the "web and woof" of all things in the World of man.

Milton in *Paradise Lost* presents Satan and Michael as the ultimate antagonists, and the Dutch Baroque playwright Vondel puts into Lucifer's mouth the words

> My mind is bent [....]
> Its certain aim, to pluck the battle-plumes
> From Michael's wings
> > (*Lucifer*, Act II, lines 590 – 592; George
> > Edmundson, trans.)

However, few observations on the scheme of things have been as profound and revealing as this quotation from "The Vision of Judgment," a controversial poem by Lord Byron:

> [...] we know
> From [the Book of] Job, that Satan hath the power to pay
> A heavenly visit thrice a-year or so [...]
> And therefore Michael and the other [i.e., Satan] wore
> A civil aspect: though they did not kiss,
> Yet still between his Darkness and his Brightness

> There passed a mutual glance of great
> politeness.
>
> (Stanzas XXXIII and XXXV; insertions
> for clarity by the editor)

Satan and Michael, though in opposition, are in toil in such a way that their duality is in fact a partnership necessary for the balance of things in the Universe.

All things in the Universe are thus kept balanced through the operation of the Law of Polarity. There is a swing to and a swing from everywhere. Yet after a certain point in either direction there comes a check, and the opposite force begins to exert itself. When the pendulum is fully to the right, the "right" is in fact at its weakest and the left takes over, gaining in momentum and power. When the pendulum is fully to the left, the "left" is in turn at its weakest, and the right takes over and swings in accelerating momentum and power. This process is present in all things, wherever they may be.

How odd that we tend to become the thing we oppose! There is a silent psychic and psychological movement in man, and, unknown to him, there is a ripening of the process and to the utter surprise of everyone he is transformed into the opposite of what he was before the climacteric. St. Paul (when he was still Saul) persecuted the early Christians with venom and hatred. He then had a sudden experience on the road to Damascus (a "photism" or "luminous phenomenon," as William James calls it in his *Varieties of Religious Experience*) that turned him completely in the reverse direction. (Acts of the Apostles 9: 1 - 22)

At this point, there also occurred the most perverse change of course in Christianity. Henceforth it was not the simple, compassionate faith of the Prophet Jesus that became Christianity, but the faith and practice of St. Paul stamped itself as the Christianity of Christ, the "Son of God" in Christian theology, a falsification that has no parallel in the history of higher religions.

We see Paul's utter restructuring of the priorities of Christianity in the New Testament itself. In Matthew 5:19, we read how Jesus stresses the commandments of maintaining Jewish law: "Whosoever therefore shall break one of these least commandments, and shall teach men so, he shall be called the least in the kingdom of heaven: but whosoever shall do and teach them, the same shall be called great in the kingdom of heaven." In his Epistle to the Romans (7: 6), Paul, in contrast to Jesus, "delivers" Christians from Jewish law: "But now we are delivered from the law, that being dead wherein we were held; that we should serve in newness of spirit, and not in the oldness of the letter."

"All Christian religious thought is shot through with the feverish spirituality of Paul," Rabbi Milton Steinberg writes ("A Mystic Note."). "It was he who imposed on it such vagaries as the corruption of the flesh, Original Sin, justification by faith alone, the incarnation, vicarious atonement and a salvation that is of individuals." Nietzsche goes so far as to state: "The life, the example, the teaching, the death of Christ, the meaning and the law of the whole gospels—nothing was left of all this after [St. Paul] had reduced it to his uses." (*The Antichrist*; H.L. Mencken, trans.) This is a view echoed by Rabbi Steinberg in his book *Basic Judaism*, for he maintains that Paul's notion of Jesus as not just a man but God incarnate as well as other key Pauline "innovations" were opposed by the early apostles, particularly by the disciples Peter and James who had known Jesus best. Thus, this view of Paul is not only an Islamic view or a Nietzschean view — it is also a mainstream Jewish view. It is at times difficult to reconcile Paul the radical iconoclast with the one who wrote of "faith, hope, charity [...] the greatest of these is charity [love]." (1 Corinthians 13: 13)

Paul's beliefs increasingly enveloped Christianity, as in the Council of Nicaea in the year 325, which began to solidify official Church views on the deity of Jesus and the Trinity (the latter a word that would soon become standard in Christianity but which no biblical writer – not even St. Paul – uses). The idea that Jesus is coeval with God is countered in the Holy Qur'an (4: 172), in which we read that Jesus was a servant of God always ready to humble himself before God. This is supported by the New Testament in Matthew, the closest of the Gospels to Jewish tradition, as it recounts Jesus' life, when we read in the Garden of Gethsemene of Jesus' submission to God as he "went a little farther, and fell on his face, and prayed, saying, 'O my Father, if it be possible, let this cup pass from me: nevertheless *not as I will, but as thou wilt*.'" (36: 29; italics by the editor).

Despite the writings of Paul and such Councils as at Nicaea, Christian traditions developed which challenged these influences. The Gnostic Gospel of Thomas, for instance, presents Jesus as a man to be emulated, not a deity to be worshiped (Elaine Pagels, *The Gnostic Gospels*).

Dr. Pagels goes on to note that—independent of knowledge of Gnostic Gospels—Christian mystics also resisted what became Christian orthodoxies. This present study, in fact, references such Christian mystics as Meister Eckhart, Jakob Böhme, Emanuel Swedenborg and William Blake, the latter of whom writes of the heritage of Jesus being in many ways falsified:

> Canst Thou forgive my blasphemy? [...]
> Seeing this False Christ, in fury and passion
> I made my voice heard all over the nation.
> ("The Everlasting Gospel")

Thus, the apostle Paul with his many epistles in the New Testament became a force for developing Christian theology on the one hand but separating such doctrine increasingly from the original teachings of Jesus on the other. Later church councils and church fathers such as St. Augustine only worked to separate Christianity further from the teachings of Jesus and the original apostles. Indeed, a further development in Christianity was that of Augustine's notion of original sin in the heart of man – notions which cause Augustine such anguish in his *Confessions*. These revisions have become so enshrined in Christianity that there is today widespread agreement among different Christian denominations about such concepts as original sin, the trinity and even salvation, though such concepts in their present form would have been utterly foreign to Jesus and his disciples.

Irrespective of the notion of original sin which developed in Christianity, most men are neither too good nor too bad in their conduct and behavior. When a catastrophe or an extreme situation violently wrenches them from their moorings, however, they tend to polarize. Some become more religious, better than before, while others turn perverse and cynical, worse than before. Why such things happen remains, in a deeper sense, inexplicable, no matter what psychological explanations are trotted out for all to see.

The functions of the human body swing back and forth with the regularity of the pendulum. The heart oscillates between systole and diastole, and we breathe in and breathe out, as seconds tick into minutes, or as the clock ticks with such precision.

The most sanctimonious hypocrites are lechers, and there are Uriah Heeps, real-life counterparts to Dickens' caricature of the falsely humble man whose other side – and his real one – is cruel, spiteful and vindictive. Man has so many such pendulums within, swinging to and fro between extremes. To the undiscerning, all this can be very confounding. Who can, however, explain the complexities of the World as it is constituted for us, humans, except the sage and the Prophet of God?

When we begin to understand this Law, we find that Time is "kept" differently at different "times." The biblical book of Ecclesiastes says: "To everything there is a season, and a time to every purpose under the heaven." (3: 1)

Ecclesiastes goes on to note that there is a time for sowing and there is a time for reaping; there is a time for play and there is a time for work; there is a time for marriage and there is a time for parenthood. What subtle nuances a day has with its pre-dawn and dawn, its forenoon and its afternoon, its evening and its dusk, its night and the watches of the night, the holy, mysterious stillness of the deeps of the majestic night with the galaxies and the constellations making their vast movements in the heavens, the awesome feeling of spirits descending and ascending and the Earth bathed in Divine refulgence.

Everything comes to an end *in time*, so that one thing is supplanted by another. If that were not so, the whole scheme of things would go awry, and no laws could operate, and no life would survive. Everything is the result of the counterbalance of two opposing forces. Remove the "counterbalance," and things will come unglued, helpless and powerless, and all "becoming" will grind to a halt. The World, as we know it, will thus be annihilated.

The Temple of the Oracle at Delphi bore two inscriptions:

Know Thyself and *Nothing Too Much*

Yet there is a "catch" in the injunction "Know Thyself." A man comes to know himself only through interaction with the world, not by detaching himself from it and cutting himself off from the stream of life. A man discovers what he actually is only through his acts and never by the mere thinking of what he is. Introspection alone leads man nowhere. Awareness and consciousness are indispensable to arrive at the truth of himself. A man arrives at the truth of himself in the bazaars, the market-places of the world, where he walks alert and aware and conscious of the impact of things on him and his impact on them. He goes through a long and arduous process of knowing and unknowing, of learning and unlearning. In the end, as the road begins to climb to the rarefied heights of the mountain, he has an inkling of who, and what he is, and his awakened self too climbs to higher states of conscious life. The mountain and the valley are part and parcel of the same landscape.

"Nothing Too Much," the other inscription of the Oracle at Delphi, is a stern warning against extremes of indulgence and denial. Proportion and balance in all things is the application of "counterbalance," the midpoint between opposites. Only a living thing is in a state of balance. To be balanced is to be *alive* to every side of life. A man cannot be alive to the nature of things at the extremes of indulgence and denial or in a fixed and rigid view of life wrapped in conceit, illusions, and self-deceptions. There is a Sufi saying: "All true life is the peace and harmony of contraries. Death is due to war between them."

This "peace and harmony of contraries" is the core and kernel of life and its mainspring. In the German tradition, this notion is echoed in Goethe's *West-östlicher Diwan,* the *Divan of West and East:*

> Im Atemholen sind zweierlei Gnaden:
> Die Luft einziehn, sich ihrer entladen.
> Jenes bedrängt, dieses erfrischt;
> So wunderbar ist das Leben gemischt.

> In the breathing art, there are two graces:
> The air inhaled, by itself releases;

The one presses, while the other eases;
How wondrously life this twain embraces.
(Mark Dreisonstok, translator)

In the esoteric teaching of the Greeks, when one opposite contends against another, a state of injustice ensues. This is happening in life, around us, all the time. The original meaning of the Greek word for "righteousness" is to be *upright*, to be midway between the opposites. Justice or righteousness was regarded as a state of balance. The just or righteous man of the Socratic and Pythagorean teachings is *the upright man*, the man who stands at midpoint between the opposites. A one-sided man, a fanatic or a bigot, could not be a just man, nor a man who was too worldly or too ascetic, nor one walking about very pleased with himself, nor one despising his own self.

An opposite encroaches on another, overcomes it and in turn it too is encroached upon and is subdued. In this continual strife, everything is contained. To pray for the end of this tension and strife is to pray for death and extinction.

The Holy Qur'an says: "For had it not been for Allah's repelling some men by means of others, cloisters and churches and oratories and mosques, wherein the name of Allah is oft mentioned would assuredly have been pulled down." (22: 40)

A ceaseless contention and strife is the immutable Law and life manifests itself in the struggle of opposing forces; order too and civilization and culture and the great movements that have shaken man in history and the profound changes that have been wrought in his life.

To pray for the end of this tension and strife is to pray for the end of things in the Universe.

Heraclitus, a highly original pre-Socratic philosopher of ancient Greece, said: "The harmony of the world is a harmony of oppositions, as in the case of the bow and of the lyre" and "The unlike is joined together and from differences results the most beautiful harmony and all things take place by strife." (G.W.T. Patrick, trans.)

The evolution of life is a brilliant case study of this Law. All species and organisms, which became perfectly adapted and stable, either died out or reached a dead-end, frozen into a blind, rigid and unchanging pattern of behavior, as is exemplified in bees and ants. Only the unstable species have evolved through tension and strife, proceeding from one unstable condition to another in an ascending direction, towards greater plasticity and freedom. Man, himself, is the supreme example.

In studying the swing of the pendulum in ourselves, we observe that we come to the same points, but often the tendency is different. Things are the same but moving in the opposite direction. We are, for instance, irritable and becoming pleasant, or pleasant and growing irritable. We are most unconscious, most "asleep," when any pendulum in us is passing the midpoint. Here it is moving the fastest and so we live, as it were, in extremes, at either end of the pendulum-swing and are not aware of what lies in the middle.

Our moods are all hung on to pendulums. We are not at all aware that real "I" is in the center of the swing. We allow ourselves to swing between excitement and dejection, between enthusiasm and depression, between over-valuation and under-valuation, between conceit and humility.

Not regarding ourselves as good, not priding ourselves on being just, not being caught by the swing of the pendulum, we come to the midpoint and we are then in a state of self-awareness. If we act from one side or the other, as when we say, "This is too much," we cannot expect anything more than the usual action-reaction swing of the opposites.

Any one-sided approach or solution has very little value. It is almost always wrong, because the spectrum of meaning, its nuances, would be totally obscured. We do not realize that an infinite range of very fine and subtle meanings is passing through us all the time. Yet as we are "asleep," they leave no trace upon our inner selves.

When we observe ourselves in the right way and include the other side, which lies in darkness, we begin to change our feeling of ourselves and realize we are both *yes* and *no* to everything. We are at first *yes* to something now and *no* to it later, or *no* to it now and *yes* to it later; or *yes* to some things and *no* to some other things, and the *yes* and *no* can interchange; or we may be *yes* and *no* at the same time, indicating a confused and contradictory state of our inner self. However: But when a contradiction caused by a buffer disappears and both sides are accepted simultaneously, a real change in our being takes place. Instead of being conscious in one side and then in the other, the two come together and become one. Then neither the one side nor the other stays as before. It is not *yes or no* but both *yes and no*. We become capable of gathering in the opposites within us; our consciousness expands to take in a sweep an in-depth and broad conception of things, leaving nothing out, no matter how opposed and contrary they may be. This is really one of the first steps towards unity of being.

We often see persons who are strongly based on *yes* to themselves and *no* to others. They are very self-opinionated. They are not aware that an opposite and contrary side exists in them. In their minds, they always tell the truth, they always do right, and they are always right. They, in fact, lack refinement and sensibility and live in a "twilight world."

Sometimes the "Moving Type" imagine they are extremely well-balanced. They cannot understand the swings of the "Emotional Type." Yet this balance may simply be the result of insensitiveness, or self-centeredness or a grossness of being.

A self-opinionated man will always be one-sided, his mind obsessed with one thing and closed to all other things. Whatever opinion he holds or expresses is the only right one to him. All others are wrong and perverse. Such men appear very satisfied with themselves. How blind and dark their lives are!

We must learn to perceive things from all sides, aspects and facets so that we may evolve and become universal in our outlook and sympathies.

The verity of this point can be illuminated if we peruse aphorisms and parables from several of the world's traditions, beginning with this insightful paradox from Chinese Taoism:

> All subjects may be looked at from (two points of view),— from that and from this. [...] This view is the same as that,

> and that view is the same as this. But that
> view involves both a right and a wrong;
> and this view involves also a right and
> a wrong. [...] They have not found their
> point of correspondency which is called
> the pivot of the Tao. As soon as one finds
> this pivot, he stands in the centre of the
> ring (of thought), where he can respond
> without end to the changing views;—
> without end to those affirming, and
> without end to those denying. – Chuang-
> Tzu (James Legge, trans.)

Similarly, Sei Shaganon remarks in her *Pillow Book* of the Japanese Heian Era of one-thousand years ago that Paradise is simultaneously near though far. More recently, in a parable related in Brazilian writer Paulo Coelho's novel *The Alchemist,* a youth first looks for meaning so near to himself that he fails to notice life around him; he later looks so far away that he spills the oil from a spoon he is holding directly in front of him. Particularly memorable is Erich Kahler's anecdote in *The Tower and the Abyss* of the Muslim and the stranger:

> A stranger saw a Muslim studying
> the Qur'an and asked: "What are you
> studying?"
> "I am studying the Qur'an", said the
> Muslim.
> "What is it about?" asked the stranger.
> "It is about God" replied the Muslim.

"Who is God?" was the stranger's next question.

"God is the Lord of the Universe," was the Muslim's answer.

"The Lord of the Universe!" wondered the stranger.

"But who is he? Where does he reside? Where is he to be seen? I only believe that to exist, which I can see with my own eyes."

The Muslim rose from his seat and went to a distance and holding the Book open asked him to read.

"How can I read if you hold the book at such a distance?" the stranger shouted in annoyance. "It is too far. I cannot see anything of the book".

The Muslim then came very close to the stranger and now held the Book so near to him that it almost touched his nose.

"Can you read now?"

"How do you expect me to read when the book is so close?" said the stranger in exasperation. "I cannot make out anything."

The Muslim countered, "Just as far and just as near as that is God."

As we see from these aphorisms and parables, great minds of a myriad of cultures and eras have attempted to break man free from seeing the world only through one prism. In life, however, almost everyone is narrow, prejudiced, smug and complacent. One man does not know or understand another. We see others through a small psychological hole, and our focus is extremely limited. This is even so with persons who pride themselves on being broad, tolerant and understanding.

The pendulum is the great deceiver within the self.

We are our states, and we cannot separate ourselves from them. We imagine a particular state to be a thing in itself that has no connection with other states. The inability to realize that it has is one reason why we find ourselves so helpless in our emotional life and so very much under its sway. It is best not to trust our feelings too much, whether they are pleasant or unpleasant. They tend to be immoderate in their expression.

Real, positive emotions could never have an opposite in them, for they can never turn negative. They may come in a flash and then disappear, but they always reveal to us what was dark to us.

The violence a man does to others sooner or later returns to him with a vengeance. Those who live by the sword "shall perish with the sword" (Matthew 26:52)— come wind, come weather. The swing of the pendulum takes care to redress the balance and settle the account.

When we say "Do unto others as you would that they do unto you"—that is, the Golden Rule—we mean to escape the operation of this Law. This is a significant point as we assay all morality, for it is one of the most universal of all ethical principles, as we see in many traditions:

Therefore all things whatsoever ye would that men should do to you, do ye even so to them: for this is the law and the prophets.

(Matthew 7: 12)

Not one of you is a believer until he loves for his brother what he loves for himself.

- Imam An-Nawawi, *Forty Hadith* (13)

What you do not want done to yourself, do not do to others.

- Confucius, *Analects* (15: 24) (James Legge, trans.)

Despite this universal plea for a moral prescription which would give human life peace and stability, it would seem that impermanence and insecurity, contention and strife are the "web and woof" of life. Health, wealth, status and power create an illusion of stability in man. In the intoxication this condition has on him he forgets that disease, loss of wealth, position and power are very real things. They may strike when he least expects them and rob him of all he has, leaving him utterly lost. Man creates his own hell.

The opposites are light and darkness, for what one is conscious of is in the light and what one is not conscious of is in the dark. These are the demonic powers, always at variance with each other. As we are, we belong to the people who live in darkness and "shun the light [like] criminals and evil spirits." (Friedrich Schiller, *Intrigue and Love*; Charles J. Hempel, trans.) We will not face ourselves, and what lies in our own darkness has a strange fascination and power over us.

Man was not created to become a slave, but he makes himself a slave to other creatures and to things and objects he craves, and blindly runs after in life. Islam has conferred upon man the supreme dignity as the vicegerent of God on earth. Yet he prostrates himself before other men and before idols of his own making, and reduces himself to a "thing" to be used and manipulated. Objects of his craving ride on him and drive him hard to all kinds of slavish acts.

"To be free" has a world of meaning. When a man thinks of the meaning of "freedom," he should ask: Freedom *for* what and freedom *from* what? *For* what does he ask to be free? *From* what does he ask to be free?

CHAPTER 15

The Nature of the Universe

Praise the name of thy Lord, the most high Who createth, then disposeth, Who measureth, then guideth.

- Holy Qur'an (87: 1-3)

He hath created everything and hath meted out for it a measure.

- Holy Qur'an (25: 2)

He (Moses) said (to Pharaoh): Our Lord is HE Who gave unto everything its nature, then guided it aright.

- Holy Qur'an (20: 50)

So set thy purpose (O Muhammad) for religion as a man by nature upright-the nature (framed) of Allah, in which He hath created man. There is no altering (the laws of) Allah's creation. That is the right religion, but most men know not.

- Holy Qur'an (Chapter 30, Verse 30)

Only knowledge of the whole is real knowledge. Knowledge of a part, without its relation to the whole is not real knowledge. It is a form of ignorance.

It is possible to acquire knowledge of the whole through the use of three principles: the principle of relativity, the principle of scale and the complementary principle, under which contradictions supplement one another and the structure of reality is raised on it. By way of illustration, thought and emotion are complementary functions, two ways of viewing the same thing.

Paradoxes, contraries and contradictions are differing aspects and facets of the world we inhabit, gather and synthesize into a unitary system of life and nature.

There is an ancient Hermetic saying: "As above, so below." What one sees on a higher scale one can see on a smaller scale. That is how everything is stamped by the Cosmic Laws through which God, the Lord of the Universe, governs everything everywhere.

Scale is a qualitative measure and covers the "above," the "below," the "higher" and the "lower" as well as the way things are interconnected on different planes and levels of Reality. Without perception of scale and levels, things appear as opposites, though they are not, and man's mind is a dichotomy of "either" and "or," leading to endless confusion and wrangles. He does not put things where they belong on the right levels on the scale. One requires a great expansion of consciousness, far beyond the so called "waking" state of man, which he believes to be full consciousness, in order to be able to *see* things at the right levels on the Cosmic Scale.

That which appears to be paradoxical and contradictory in the ordinary state of consciousness ceases to he so under the world-view of the principle of scale and the complementary principle. Then things fall on their own into their proper place in the light of a higher conscious state of man. An intuitive perception or understanding of the nature of things—with all the contraries, contradictions and complementary order, resolves them into a harmonious whole. Man then is enabled to think in different categories and orders and view them on the right levels on the Cosmic Scale.

The Universe, which is the Macrocosm, is a vast and stupendous network of hierarchical orders, levels and planes in the Cosmic Scale, utterly defying man's weak and feeble power of comprehension. Man himself, as a microcosm, stands on different levels and planes on the human scale, and to take all men as similar (on the same level and order) is merely a sign of a very undeveloped consciousness and a pitiable understanding.

We are living and breathing in a related Universe, in which everything is related to every other thing and each thing exerts its own force—weak or strong—on all the rest. Nothing can be taken separately, isolated from the rest. Nothing can ever exist independently of any other thing. Yet each object in the Universe, at its level and plane on the Scale, has its own particular place and existence in the Cosmic Order, although it is connected with what is above it and what is below it. "As above, so below."

All forces on whatever level, plane or order they exist, again come under the so called Law of Affinity and the Law of Polarity, of attraction and repulsion. Like attracts like. Unlike repels unlike. Tension and strife of opposing forces hold them in balance and proportion. Love, tension, contention and strife are the eternal forces, the building blocks of the Universe. Disorder gives birth to order, and order eventually runs into disorder. These contending forces are never at rest; there is a churning and a turning and a vast sweep of movement, up and down, far and near, east and west (though these so called "directions" have no meaning in Cosmic Space).

"Polytheist" man forgets that God does not govern the Universe by capricious decrees. He has created particular and general Laws which are then imposed upon all phenomena in Nature, a certain order of succession and behavior, of balance and proportion, of evolution and devolution. All phenomena unroll in the directions irrevocably ordained for them. When a phenomenon is set going, it must inevitably traverse a certain course, until a moment arrives when the conditions are altered in such a manner that other laws take over the direction.

Laws are multiple, ascending in an hierarchical order to general laws, encompassing the whole Cosmos. There are particular laws, which regulate the different objects of Nature, as for instance the germination of a seed or the birth, growth and death of a cell: how a seed grows into a specific plant or tree bearing a particular flower or fruit; how the different cells in an organism become differentiated from the original cell and acquire their specific properties and characteristics. All laws are immutable. Man does not know the "why" of these processes. They have remained a teasing and yet awesome mystery to him.

Even chance, probability and unaccountable fluctuations operate under certain laws and principles, dark to man at the level of his understanding. He remains ignorant of why these things happen in the manner which they do.

Differing conditions produce new and varying phenomena in Reality. It is the scale of observation or the frame of reference that matters in a crucial sense. With every change in the scale or the frame of reference, new phenomena come to manifest themselves. The relativity of every aspect observed, according to the *place* it occupies in the Cosmic Order, must be clearly comprehended.

There pervades through all the laws an awesome and harmonious majesty, knit together into one indivisible Whole and revealing God's infinite power and wisdom.

All manifestations of energy, whether in Nature or in human affairs, whether internal or external, are the creation of three forces. They may be called "positive," "negative" and "synthetic." There is a difference in their mode of operation, and it is this difference that causes all the infinite variety of phenomena in Nature. These three forces always work in unison, but their combinations would vary in every triad. What is positive in one triad at one moment may become negative or synthetic in another triad at some other moment or phase, but in any combination, one force will always be dominant. "Triads" refer to all events and situations in nature and human affairs. The "synthetic" force acts as a catalyst. Things manifest themselves only when all the three forces come together to work in combination. Nothing will happen if they do not come together, and two forces cannot produce any result, unless there is a catalyst to bind them. They will just spin around each other without resolution.

It takes insight and understanding to observe the working of these three forces in all things. For some unfathomable reason, we are blind to the "synthetic" force, even though we observe it in many chemical reactions and biological phenomena. We do not observe clearly the inter-play of two forces but, surprisingly enough, expect things to happen when only one force is present.

Each force modifies the other two in their inter-play so that, in the final outcome, the end is never the one which had been originally anticipated or planned.

It is not the thing, object, event or situation itself but the force it conducts at a given moment that is crucial. Love makes us see an object in one way, hate in quite a different way. It is the same object, yet it conducts different forces at different times.

There are persons who make difficulties about almost everything. Nearly everyone has an attribute in his being which is the dominant trait in his character. It is like a central axle round which everything in a man turns. It is this particular attribute that is the ultimate factor in every decision reached. Yet this factor also makes for the greatest "negative" force in him.

> This attribute may be a weak will, a grudge against the world, envy, indecisiveness, avarice, vanity, selfishness, lust, resentment, intolerance, bigotry, narrow-mindedness and a thousand obsessive feelings man is wrapped in, one particular trait that mars his life. Putting this in a Shakespearean context, it is the tragic flaw which leads man to his ultimate downfall or failure.
>
> Such flaws of character are on display in this scene from Shakespeare's Macbeth:

First Murderer: We are men, my liege.

Macbeth: Ay, in the catalogue ye go for men;
    As hounds and greyhounds, mongrels,
    spaniels, curs,
    Shoughs, water-rugs and demi-
    wolves; are clept
    All by the name of dogs: the valu'd file
    Distinguishes the swift, the slow, the
    subtle,
    The housekeeper, the hunter,
    every one
    According to the gift which bounteous
    nature
    Hath in him clos'd; whereby he does
    receive
    Particular addition, from the bill
    That writes them all alike: and so
    of men.
    Now, if you have a station in the file,
    Not i' the worst rank of manhood,
    say it;
    And I will put that business in your
    bosoms.
    Whose execution takes your
    enemy off,
    Grapples you to the heart and love
    of us,
    Who wear our health but sickly in his
    life,
    Which in his death were perfect.

Second Murderer: I am one, my liege,
>Whom the vile blows and buffets of the world
>Have so incens'd that I am reckless what I do to spite the world.

First Murderer: And I another
>So weary with disasters, tugg'd with fortune,
>That I would set my life on any chance,
>To mend it or be rid on 't.
>>(Act III, Scene I)

Macbeth, who in some ways embodies praiseworthy virtues such as great courage, is here ready to commit murder, ordering the murderers to kill his friend Banquo, whom the Weird Sisters predicted would (instead of Macbeth) be "father to a line of kings" (Act III, Scene I). Banquo's son is also the intended victim of this plot. All this is done by Macbeth in order to keep the throne of Scotland for himself and his future heirs. Yet the seeds of Macbeth's tragic flaw of unbounded ambition are already revealed in his character in Act I, Scene I, in which the main character of Shakespeare's "Scottish play" states:

I have no spur
To prick the sides of my intent, but only
Vaulting ambition, which o'erleaps itself
And falls on th' other.

Macbeth would have done well to have been on guard against this negative trait in his character which ultimately brings about his downfall.

A succession of events proceeds in accordance with another law of nature. Under it, no force ever works continuously in the same direction. After a certain time, it weakens in energy, and one of two things happens to it. It may change its direction or it may undergo a transformation. We can observe the operation of this law in human affairs. When persons commence some work, the momentum leads it on, and then it slows down for no apparent reason. If, at that moment, an extra "push" were not given, the line of work imperceptibly veers to another direction, with a significant change in its force and strength. It slackens again at another psychological moment, and—unless an extraordinary effort is injected—the thing takes a diametrically opposed course, although on the surface it may still appear to be the same thing. Everyone involved in the process of work may remain deceived.

All evolutionary development is spiral. This opens the way, as nothing else can, for an intelligent being to gather in a rich harvest of experience in its passage forward towards evolution of the personal self. As it climbs in its spiral staircase, it descends as it ascends; it gains as it loses, and there is a thrust upward, uneven and intermittent though it may appear. Every ascent in the cyclic arc is higher, reaching towards a greater degree of intelligence, plasticity, freedom and consciousness.

Matter is synonymous with energy, which vibrates in a space-time continuum. Everything in the Universe is affected by every other thing. Man's imagination staggers at the thought of the wondrous and awesome nature of the Cosmos, that stupendous indivisible field of vibrations, as galaxies and constellations majestically whirl and wheel in the limitless interstellar spaces. The organic life on this very tiny planet, the Earth, is just a thin film covering its crust and serves as a transmitting apparatus for cosmic radiations.

CHAPTER 16

The Teachings of Sages, Prophets and Philosophers

There is not a people but a warner (prophet) hath passed among them.
                          - Holy Qur'an (35: 24)

To every people we sent a prophet to teach them to worship God and to avoid evil. Some of them were rightly guided, others erred and were rightly punished. Go unto the nations and see to what end those who erred had come.
                          - Holy Qur'an (16: 36)

So set thy purpose (O Muhammad) for religion as a man by nature upright - the nature (framed) of Allah, in which He hath created man. There is no altering (the laws of) Allah's creation. That is the right religion, but most men know not.
                          - Holy Qur'an (30: 30)

A prophet has come to every people to teach them one and the same truth. The teaching has varied in form and presentation to suit the age and the special condition or milieu of each community. The object was to establish the worship of one supreme God, free from all traces of polytheism. Each prophet came to teach man to walk upright in his life, to recognize that, as the creature of God, he should worship God alone and never allow himself to worship any object in creation which itself has been created by God. Yet there have been misinterpretations of the teachings of sages, prophets and philosophers. The creators of great works of literature and the founders of the great faiths of mankind were followed by their interpreters, at first the disciples and later disciples of the disciples and then a long line of critics, all giving their own versions and interpretations to the words and the works of the Masters. There have been wars of words and wars to kill and impose particular interpretations.

The true Path of God was to confer upon man his unique dignity as a human being, slave to no one, *no mere thing* to be used and manipulated by powers of darkness, belonging to Him alone, as His vicegerent on Earth. The aim and purpose of the Teaching was to transform man from his ordinary, mechanical state into a fully developed person. Most, however, chose to remain wayward, perverse and obdurate in their ways, preferring to exist as creatures of other creatures of God, unmindful of how this violated their human dignity. They chose to dwell in darkness. Only a few heeded the prophet's message and obeyed his call to God.

To understand the meaning of the Teaching, man has to rid himself of false notions, that is, to free himself from the shackles of tradition and artificial social values and conventions and age-old customs. He has to cultivate the right attitude to and the right relationship with all that is outside him. The crux is to know and conform to the fundamental order of things, the nature framed of God, immutable and unalterable, and never to violate it. This Teaching of the fundamental order of things coalesces in Islam, the eternal religion taught to man by God's prophets.

Mechanical man takes this Teaching too in a mechanical manner, content to observe the outward forms and rituals, to take the literal meaning of the Teaching and to distort it so that the original is completely obscured. He has a strange habit of taking truth in its "outward" sense and perverting it to ignoble and base uses and ends. People are told to believe, to ask no questions and to do without understanding. Then grace, mercy and charity pass away and dogmas, rituals and rigid interpretations close their intolerant grip on human affairs. The few who know and dare to call things by their proper name are maligned and persecuted until they are silenced forever. The tyranny of literal truth and opinion is the most terrible of all tyrannies. As Goethe says,

> [...] Who may dare
> To name things by their real names?
> The few
> Who did know something, and were weak enough
> To expose their hearts, unguarded - to expose
> Their views and feelings to the eyes of men.
> They have been nailed to crosses - thrown to flames.
>
> - *Faust, Part I* (John Anster, trans.)

If Scripture says that God, in His anger, casts a man down in hell, to one man who is outwards turned it appears to mean literally what it says. For another man, who can see both the outer and the inner meaning of things, this takes on an inner sense and means that a man casts himself down to a very low and wretched spiritual condition when he is in an evil state. Both are viewing the same thing, but with two different minds, and thus they receive totally different impressions of it. The man who is external in his outlook has been the enemy of God, man and, perversely, himself in the end. Satan, that power of negation, could not ask for a more malleable disciple than the man who only looks at outward appearance.

The religion of God uses parable, symbol, allegory, similitude and paradox to describe states and conditions of man in his quest for God and the meaning of things. It is not possible to describe higher states of conscious experience in ordinary language, which is really a function of the level of "things seen." (Hebrews 11:1)

The history of religious ideas is a history of their misuse and misinterpretation when they pass into ordinary, external life. They then become sources of political intrigue, violence, persecution and wars.

> And verily we have displayed for mankind
> all manner of similitudes,
> but man is more than anything contentious.
> - Holy Qur'an (18: 55)

We speak of "bliss" in paradise and "torment" in hell. They are spiritual states and conditions man has earned in his life on earth. To be free from "fear, grief and pain," in the words of the Holy Qur'an, is to experience real "pleasure" or "bliss," which is the quality and texture of paradise. No one can ever experience this "real pleasure" if he has not merited it. Then he is subject to "fear, grief and pain," which is a condition of hell.

It is a law of life that everything has a price, and unless the right price is paid, one does not obtain the thing one prizes and desires. Such payment is never easy.

We must realize how often we are governed and controlled not by the things themselves, but by our imagination and fantasy of them. We can deceive ourselves about anything, for we are too easily taken in by the empty gloss and glitter of the world, forgetting that "all that is of the earth, shall turn to earth again." (Ecclesiasticus 41:10)

No one ever does evil wittingly. Everyone acts for "good" as he understands it, and everyone understands it in his own way, depending on which rung of the ladder of "being" he stands. To the lover, his beloved is beautiful and most desirable, no matter how she appears to others. She may be odious to them. Erasmus expresses this truth in humorous terms in his bright Renaissance work *In Praise of Folly*:

> And now tell me if to wink, slip over, be
> blind at, or deceived in the vices of our
> friends, nay, to admire and esteem them
> for virtues, be not at least the next
> degree to folly? What is it when one kisses
> his mistress' [...] wart on her nose?
> When a father shall swear his squint-eyed
> child is more lovely than Venus? What
> is this, I say, but mere folly?
>
> (John Wilson, trans.)

A foul odor is not foul according to its own nature, for it is fragrance itself unto itself. An evil thing is good in itself to itself and regards good as evil from its perch, just as to the man who attends to human excreta, the foul odor does not offend, so used does he become to it. If he were suddenly to inhale a fragrant perfume, he would not be able to "tolerate" it and perhaps fall unconscious. Men cheat, lie, deceive, hurt, torture, persecute and murder one another for "good," according to their own perception. The cause is the spiritual blinkers they wear, their ignorance of the nature of things or their perverseness and obduracy, that is, the state of "unreality" in which they pass their lamentable existence.

In the language of the Holy Qur'an:

> Or as darkness on a vast, abysmal sea.
> There covereth him a wave, above which
> is a wave, above which is a cloud. Layer
> upon layer of darkness. When he holdeth
> out his hand he scarce can see it. And he
> for whom Allah hath not appointed light,
> for him there is no light.
>
> - "Light," Holy Qur'an (24: 40)

If a man has faith in one kind of life and lives another, what, then, is he?

The world has such a fatal charm and hold on man that he would never want to leave it if it were left to his choice, but man is ultimately a solitary, tragic figure. Death at last snatches him away and brings to naught all his ambitions and desires. He comes into the world alone. He finally goes out of it alone, forced to abandon everything and to be abandoned, willy-nilly, by all. The very thought of death scares and indeed terrifies him. He refuses to realize that he has to come to terms with it, if his life is to be lived rightly and well. Death is, after all, the other side of life, and life depends on death, just as death depends on life. To learn to know what death is is to learn to know what life is and how it has to be lived. Every man gives his own meaning to life as he lives it, and this meaning is derived paradoxically from death. A man awakens when he dies and then knows things as they really are. No one may reap what he has not sown. (Galatians 6: 7) A man is raised up in the state in which he has died, and he dies in the state in which he has lived. "Whoso is blind here will be blind in the hereafter and yet further from the path." (Holy Qur'an, 17: 72)

Every moment we are enveloped by cosmic forces, from the living magnetism of the stars to the loving kindness of God. The only appropriate response is to do our duty, as has fallen to our lot, the best we can and to see things with the inner eye, to listen with the inner ear and to feel and understand with the warm, throbbing heart, ever sensitive to the beat and rhythm of things.

The more objective we are the clearer is our understanding of dynamic Reality and of our own selves, *as they are, in their suchness*, and not as distorted by private desires and fears.

True humility is that which does not luxuriate in the feeling of oneself. Great simplicity distinguishes true humility.

Man has always hankered after wages, which take many forms and shapes. He expects reward and recognition, riches and honors, fame and adulation. He even expects "paradise" for the selfish prayers he makes to his "god." Yet he is never conscious of the debts he owes to others. The most difficult thing is to learn how to pay, and indeed we have to pay for each and everything, but we think others owe us and we owe them nothing. In order to move forward, it is imperative that we take care to pay off all our debts, and that means we have to put every relationship right and to redress every wrong we have ever done.

CHAPTER 17

The True Nature of Will

For Schopenhauer, the notion of *Wille* led him to Pessimism; Nietzsche spoke of the "Will to Power." These and other philosophers have spoken of and defined the will in different ways, but they may have had only an imperfect understanding of the will.

The gravity of human will is in the Emotional Center. The more this Center is refined, the higher is the will; the more gross and crude it is, the lower is the will, for will is a new insight, very quiet, flexible and discerning and transcending all self-wills. Its basis is *positive* emotion, and active patience is the mother of this will.

There are many meanings to every single thing. The beginning of the growth of will is to see nuances of meaning, facets and aspects where before one saw only one thing or just contrasting opposites.

It takes a long time to understand that doing what we desire does not give us any freedom. Self-will does not lead to satisfaction, nor does self-indulgence, which—like indigence—is an extreme form of wretchedness. Inner freedom does not mean gratifying the desire of the moment, for this would really be slavery of the impulse. Indeed, what could be darker or more murkier than self-impulse or heedlessness?

> Hast thou seen the man who makes *self-impulse* his god?
>
> > - Holy Qur'an (23: 45)

As perception, insight and understanding grow, *will* develops, and inner freedom is realized. We cannot expect to have any degree of inner freedom if we are under the sway of impulses. Our feelings are unreal, and we find ourselves at the mercy of every change, chance, incident or event in external life. We are buffeted by our impulses and scattered in all directions by them. Self-will breeds impulses and then to regard ourselves as a free agent of our acts is to call a slave a free man, but it is we who bind and truss ourselves and yet consider ourselves free.

A man usually makes an aim from a small side of himself and forgets about it soon after, for his self-wills pull him in various directions, and his attention roves here, there, everywhere. He tries to alter one thing without knowing how it is connected with other things. This just shows that he makes only mechanical decisions. His life passes "rounded in a sleep," as Shakespeare phrases it in *The Tempest*, in a state of unreality, in bondage to incidents and events that overwhelm him. He rarely makes an aim or decision that does not, in some way or other, depend on some other person's approval or support. This means he does things usually with an admixture of "being seen of men." (Matthew 6: 5)

We can keep an aim only when our consciousness and will coalesce. Will arises in being, and it is a man's level of being that eventually decides what he does. He may decide to act in a certain way, but when the moment comes, his level of being causes him to act in a quite different way. It is only when an aim is made consciously, with insight, from will, after a long and careful study, that it gives shape, meaning and direction to a man's inner life. It liberates him from the mechanical state. He becomes a more conscious person, and he opens himself to an understanding of Reality.

Merely to see a thing is true is not enough. A man has to see the good of the truth and *will* it. Truth then becomes connected with his inner life and is made vibrant and living.

There is a dispensation in the affairs of man, which is of a disquieting meaning and import. At some moment in a man's life there may intervene, all of a sudden, without a sign or warning, a mysterious decree between his heart and his will. His life then gets deflected from good to evil or from evil to good. A profound change has supervened in his character. The evil and harm that he intended to commit, before the climacteric, is suddenly abandoned—just as the good that he meant to do is as suddenly dropped.

A slow, silent, unconscious process of psychological change may have been going on in the inner life of the man, and—at some moment—it ripens and bursts into the open, only to leave everyone mystified.

Man lives on the brink of a precipice, and he has to be very watchful over his internal states, lest some unforeseen event or situation may throw him headlong to his doom. The nearer a man is to his ruin, the less he realizes the seriousness of his perilous condition.

> Is he who founded his dwelling upon duty
> toAllah and His good
> pleasure better; or he who founded his
> house on the brink of a crumbling,
> overhanging precipice so that it toppled
> with him into the fire of hell?
>
> > - Holy Qur'an (9: 109)

Everything in a man can only grow through his own will and understanding that things must be what they are. They cannot be any different or other than what they are. The fundamental order of things imposes its irrevocable conditions, and man's life should never deviate from the Laws set for all objects in the Cosmic Scheme.

There is no yardstick to measure a human being. He carries within him seeds of growth as well as germs of death and decay.

It is an extraordinary experience to know what is real in oneself, for whatever is real in a man is unique to him, possessed by no one else. This is the most extraordinary thing about man: whatever he is or becomes is how he has applied his will and understanding, the direction he has given his own life.

As long as a man is *life-directed*, unlike one who directs his own life, he has no will of his own. His one consuming desire is to possess and enjoy the things of this world. We must not forget that will is a spiritual force, ever aspiring towards God.

CHAPTER 18

Self-awareness and Consciousness

> Is he who was dead and we have raised
> him into life and set for him a light
> wherein he walketh amongst men, be like
> unto him who is in the depths of darkness
> from whence he cannot emerge.
>
> - Holy Qur'an (6: 123)

Jakob Böhme was a great mystic and a rare person by any measure. A German Christian theologian who lived between 1575 and 1624, he was a believer in the inner light and illumination:

> At the age of twenty-five he was
> surrounded by the divine light, and
> replenished with the heavenly knowledge;
> insomuch as going abroad into the fields
> to a green, at Görlitz, he there sat down,
> and viewing the herbs and grass of the
> field, in his inward light he saw into their
> essences, use, and properties, which was
> discovered to him by their lineaments,
> figures, and signatures.
>
> - William James, "Mysticism," Lectures
> 16 and 17, *The Varieties of Religious
> Experience*

To Böhme, all existence implied opposition, and good could be known only in opposition to evil: out of the conflict of opposites, unity came into being.

> A disciple once asked him how he could attain "the supersensual life and hear God speak."
>
> Böhme replied: "When thou canst throw thyself into that, where no creature dwelleth, though it be for a moment, then thou hearest what God speaketh."
>
> The disciple queried: "Master, is the place far or near?"
>
> The Master said: "It is in thee, when thou standest still from self-thinking and self-willing and canst stop the wheel of imagination and the senses.
>
> - *The Supersensual Life*

A Persian Sufi put it this way: "I went in and left myself outside." Another Sufi likened higher conscious experience to rising to the surface of the sea to draw in air. "The air," he wrote some eight centuries ago, "is miraculous and will last a whole day, even when one is at the bottom of the sea." (The reader is directed to Martin Lind's *What is Sufism?* for more on Sufism, the mystical strain of Islam which is in some ways akin to Böhme's Christian mysticism.)

A man then comes into a new reality of his being and perceives everything in a new relationship. He sees things with the eye of the heart, and things do not appear as separate entities. There is a web of relationships among objects whose meanings derive entirely from their relationship to the whole. Objects and events are really patterns in a Cosmic process. This vision to the eye of the heart in profound stillness of being is a revelation of the nature of things as they are bathed in a Divine glow or "celestial light," as Wordsworth has it in "Ode to Intimations of Immortality from Recollections of Early Childhood."

A man must try to establish a distinct awareness of where he is inside himself, though as Lucretius writes:

> So each man strives to flee that secret foe
> Which is himself. But move he swift or slow,
> That Self, for ever punctual at his heels,
> Never for one short hour will let him go.
> (*On the Nature of Things*, Book III, 1081-1083; W.H. Mallock, trans.)

Yet psychologically, we are most what we nourish most, and we nourish most what we love most. What a man values highest or loves most is really "God" for him—and what strange "gods" do men worship! Nonetheless, man imagines he loves God more than anything else. How difficult it is to notice one's own deceptions and illusions! Everything hinges on relationship in how one relates oneself to objects and events. One cannot change an object or an event, but one can change one's relationship to it. In the words of D.H. Lawrence:

> When I stand with another man, who is himself, and when I am truly myself, then

> I am only aware of a Presence, and of the
> strange reality of Otherness. There is me,
> and there is another being [...] There is no
> comparing or estimating. - *Phoenix*

Self-awareness can be reached in various ways in keeping
with the differing conditions of life at different moments:

> Would a man get out of his own way?
> Would he still the mind even for a
> moment?
> Would he detach himself from the
> ordinary feeling of himself?
> Would he become *no one* to himself for a
> moment?

Or:

> Would he *feel* the intense reality of
> himself?
> Would he *feel* the real "I" in his work for
> a time?

The question of all questions is: How does one *awaken*
to another, higher level of reality? This is the crux of a
conscious life.

God speaks to us in the depth of stillness. Yet the mind
is never still; it is ever restless. In our ignorance, we believe
that to "still" the mind is to make one mindless. We really
dread silence. We cannot bear to live with our own inner
selves, for silence reveals to us the awful emptiness that
darkens our inner self.

The spiritual power of silence is best illustrated in the first "silent sermon" of Sayyadana Osman when he succeeded Sayyadana Omar as the third Caliph. He mounted the pulpit and sat there "utterly silent" in the words of Moulana Room, the supreme mystical poet in world literature:

> He looked steadily at the people and caused a state of ecstasy to descend upon them. A great awe sat on the assembly; the court and roof of the mosque were filled with the light of God. He who had seeing eyes was beholding God's light.

Very few know the art of silence. We can keep silence in such a way that it would not be noticed, and this silence gives us an inner feeling of strength and integrity. It is only through the way of inner silence that we discover not only our real self, but also reach higher conscious life. This silence has its own tone and quality, and we who say a great deal too much would never understand or realize its significance and value. Not only do we talk too much; we tend to overstep the limit in everything, whether it be food, drink, sex, work, play or useless occupations. With everything, there is a limit to what is necessary. Wisdom is to know what that is, yet man ever transgresses and goes beyond the limit man just transgresses. He attaches more importance to the superfluous than he does to the "necessary." His ego delights in superfluities. Everything that is superfluous or unnecessary goes to put a man to "sleep," or what is called *ghaflah* in Arabic. The root of man's contumacy and obduracy is this very "sleep" or *ghafla*.

Man is his own greatest enemy. He is much too anxious to improve his circumstances and all-too-slack to improve himself. Suffering comes to him as he chases ends that are really expressions of his ignorance and blindness. The moment of fulfillment or surfeit is the birth of an indefinable unease, pang, anxiety or remorse. Man ascribes ultimacy to the wrong things, and his vain pursuit turns into an alien power that destroys him in the end. Even to give up things will be of no avail, for the source of human misery, the very heart of human distress, is not the thing craved for, but the "craving" itself. Unless this is dispensed with, man can never break through the prison of his lusts and worldly desires, or rather his impulses.

It is certainly not at all reprehensible for a man to enjoy the good things of life in wise moderation, taking care not to violate the sense of human dignity. Satisfaction of sane and healthy pleasures in the appropriate context enriches life, while barren asceticism or mortification impoverishes it. Any excess indicates an imbalance and a loss of right proportion. The individual goes wrong when he becomes possessive and is obsessed by the very desire itself to enjoy things. This becomes servitude of the appetites and the base impulses.

> Say, who hath forbidden the adornment of
> God, which He brought forth
> for His creatures and the good things of
> His providing?
>
> - Holy Qur'an (7: 32)

Say: My Lord forbiddeth only indecencies,
such of them as are apparent,
and such as are within and sin and
wrongful oppression.

- Holy Qur'an (7: 33)

Everyone has a central ground of being in him. This is his real "I." Yet the impact of sensory impressions is so powerful and "hypnotic" that he gets very far from this center. Self-awareness is the beginning of the effort to bring him back to it. At the same time, a very external man would find it very difficult to understand what self-awareness means. He believes he already possesses it. He would consider any attempt at self-awareness as a sheer waste of time and, ultimately, foolishness.

Were a man, in his ordinary state, to experience a moment of full awareness or consciousness, he would lose his sanity and identity, because all his inner contradictions would be mercilessly exposed to him. It requires very long and arduous work on oneself to reach such a degree of insight and understanding.

The Delphic inscription "Know thyself" (γνῶθι σεαυτόν, or transliterated: Gnothi Seauton) is not the beginning of a man's journey into himself. It is the end of it, for if to know oneself were so easy, it would not have been put as a demand. By itself, it leads nowhere, for everyone thinks he knows himself.

The most damaging illusion is man's feeling that he knows himself. This is the root of the reason why he is satisfied with himself as he is. If he is not, he puts the blame on others or on circumstances. Most of us remain ignorant of ourselves all our life. We do get occasional furtive impressions of our real selves, but we dismiss the uncomfortable feeling that rocks us for a moment by taking shelter behind plausible excuses, and soon we return to our previous condition and resume our habitual ways.

Man is much more complex than he need be just to exist. He has within him a marvelous capacity to evolve to higher states of conscious life. Unless there is a psychological transformation in him, living a more conscious life, the past will create the future, and the future will be like the past. It has to be so because a man's reception of life and its situations and events will always produce the same mechanical results.

Thomas Traherne (1636-1674), a British poet with mystical tendencies, probing his innermost being in a moment of higher conscious experience, revealed in *Centuries of Meditations*: "[Y]ou will not believe, how I was withdrawn from all endeavours of altering and mending outward things."

Self-awareness has been described in an ancient book thus: "I come out of everything else into myself." This would appear at first glance to contradict the Persian Sufi's mystic drenched words: "I went in and left myself outside." On a deeper level, however, there is no contradiction, for self-awareness is the early stage of "conscious life." It is a voyage of discovery of man's real self. Many stages have to be attained and many stations to be reached before a man could utter the cryptic words: "I went in and left myself outside." These higher states are a revelation of the nature of things as they are, a man's own self witnessing them. He is bathed in Divine light. It is "Light" that he at last comes to possess, the light that reveals to him the ultimate nature of things. This is the last station of the mystic experience. Even then man, by nature and constitution, is incapable of "seeing" God. No created thing throughout the entire Cosmos can ever stand the "vision" of God.

To become "conscious" is to see entirely new relations. In the ordinary life we live, in times of trouble and distress, we may begin to "see" things in a new light or look about us and exclaim: "How strange! Why am *I* here!" Alternately, it may come to us at a highly charged emotional moment or when we find ourselves in extreme danger. We then hear our own voice and observe ourselves as if we were a third person.

Just as a fish lives in water, we humans live in a world of meanings. We are immersed in meanings, and yet we are little aware of these meanings, just as the fish is not aware of the water. We have strayed far from the significance of these meanings. We project into every object, event and situation of life the poor and inadequate meanings by which we live. None of us can grow and evolve until we reach a stage of development which enables us to *see* the finer, subtler and deeper meanings in things. Psychologically, we all live in a multi-dimensional world, and yet how odd and strange it is that the superficial life we inhabit is not even Three-Dimensional. Depth is height, and height is depth. For most of us, there is no depth or height. It is just plain length and breadth. Man, the apex of created things, has become a creature not of God, but of the other "creatures" which he has come to worship. As such, he does not walk upright in the sense that he has not developed his full potential as a human being.

Consciousness is a synthesis of perception, insight, intuition and understanding, and a higher level of conscious experience is characterized by a larger synthesis. Conscience, by analogy and also by contrast, is a drawing together of feelings and emotions into a unity of our affective life. It is a state in which a man cannot hide anything from his own self. Yet its intimation is so low-key and difficult for all but the most sensitive of humans to perceive that most of us do not heed its promptings. The psychological evolution of man is the synthetic fusion of consciousness and conscience, interacting on each other in balance and proportion. When this measure is reached, man begins to evolve to higher states and levels, vertical to the horizontal life which he leads.

Socrates stated in the Platonic dialogue *Phaedo*:

> ... the soul too is then dragged by the body into the region of the changeable, and wanders and is confused; the world spins round her, and she is like a drunkard when under their influence... when returning into herself she reflects; then she passes into the realm of purity, and eternity, and immortality, and unchangeableness, which are her kindred, and with them she ever lives, when she is by herself and is not let or hindered; then she ceases from her erring ways, and being in communion with the unchanging is unchanging.... this state of the soul is called wisdom...
>
> (Benjamin Jowett, trans.)

Man has lost his way. His soul has become immersed in outer things: in power, status, money, possessions, fame and name. The soul must turn around to find its right direction and so restore to man the meanings and realities he has lost.

Only a few seek within themselves. Man lives for and looks towards the future, which he should dread, for this construct of thinking is taking him to his grave. In his youth, fresh in vigor and vitality, man worries – indeed, *longs* – for "To-morrow's Silence, Triumph, or Despair," which he should dread, for this construct of thinking is taking him where "we too into the Dust descend." (Omar Khayyam, *Rubáiyát,* LXXIV and XXIV; Edward FitzGerald, trans.) Death for the average man is something that always happens to others, as he shuts out the idea of his own death from his consciousness.

Most famously it was Lucretius who pin-pointed the fear of death to be an essential cause of human suffering:

> Oh you who under silken curtains lie,
> And you whose only roof-tree is the sky,
> What is the curse that blights your lives alike?
> Not that you hate to live, but fear to die.
> (*On the Nature of Things*, Book III, 1078-
> 1080; W.H. Mallock, trans.)

Until man refuses to face reality objectively and realize that this life of his has all its worth and meaning only when he has learnt to die to himself (that is, to purge himself of all selfish desires), all remains a mocking, empty and futile thing. Only a few seek within themselves.

Although it is true that our perception of life changes at differing moments in our lives, we have to have the insight and subtle understanding to realize that it has been in fact constant, despite the appearance of change.

Man's contact with reality is tenuous, and most of what he takes for reality is merely a mirage. He is a stranger to himself, and everyone else is a stranger to him. He is actually a shriveled fragment of a man, unaware of what is real in him or what is real in the world outside of him.

To know reality is to embark on a journey inwards of the interior life, a "path to the inner self," in Hesse's words. Veil after veil of illusions and self-deceptions have to be penetrated in order to reach the "light" from the outer darkness of false appearances and values. A man then is enabled to see into himself and the objective world *as they truly are*. In this deep act of *seeing*, layered with intuitive insight, the division of subject and object disappears, and they are seen flowing into each other as aspects of the same process. He reaches a very high conscious state, and in that moment it is revealed to him the meaning of the love of God, for this love is a tremendous thing and very far from the ordinary idea man has of it. A blade of grass then comes to him as a revelation of the wonder and mystery of all creation. He is possessed by the feeling of awe, the most sublime feeling man can experience.

How can a man, living within only a small part of himself, "asleep" in the senses—mean, petty, selfish and hypocritical—know or understand what the love of God is, especially if that man looks down on another and rejects him because he is of a different race or color, class or creed? He may love his own notion of God, the God he worships; that is subjective, and if someone were to disagree with him, he might harm, injure or kill him.

What we call "love" can turn into hatred in a moment. True love is a positive emotion which can never turn into its opposite because it *includes* all opposites. There can be no development of love without a development of consciousness.

At the level of a higher conscious state which we have yet to attain, the sense of what is important and what is unimportant will be utterly different. To some individuals, it comes as a flash of vision, and in that moment they are beyond any awareness of time. Troubles, cares and anxieties fall away and lie far below them. Things are wondrously luminescent in all their depths. This is when human beings feel their personal existence as intensely real almost for the first time.

Alfred Lord Tennyson recorded of himself:

> A kind of waking trance I have frequently had, quite up from boyhood, when I have been alone. This has generally come upon me through repeating my name two or three times to myself, silently, till all at once, as it were, out of the intensity of the consciousness of individuality, the individuality itself seemed to fade away into boundless being and this not a confused state, but the clearest of the clearest, the surest of the surest, utterly beyond words, when death was almost a laughable impossibility (if so it were)

seeming no extinction but only true life.
[...] I am ashamed of my feeble description.
Have I not said that the state is beyond
words?

(Cited by Hallam Lord Tennyson
in *Tennyson, A Memoir*, 2 vols.
[London,1897],1:320)

Just as waking makes dreams unreal, so does waking
to another level of consciousness make all our ordinary
problems and perplexities seem unreal. This is so because
our lives are governed by a false set of values. There is
no awareness of a higher reality in our lives, and we are
reminded how far away from reality we live and that we
only dwell in the shadow of shadows.

If we could see all the relations and affinities that
an object embodies simultaneously, we would be on the
supra-mental level of conscious experience. The world
would then present itself to us in an entirely new light. We
would perceive the links and inter-connections and realize
the meaning and significance of the things we perceive,
those which are above and those which are below in the
Cosmic Scale, their mutual attractions and repulsions and
their rhythmic relationships.

Each person has his own individual line of development,
and what may be easy for one may be difficult for another.
Yet just where a man has been helped becomes the most
difficult place he has to help himself, for "help" is a very
deceptive and slippery notion. In one case, the man is
propelled up, for he possesses insight and understanding,
and in another he is pushed down, for he is too dependent

and lacks insight and understanding. In the "Prologue in Heaven" of *Faust*, Goethe likens man to a grasshopper, flying through space upwards for the sublime and falling to earth burying himself in the soiled earth:

> ... he to me
> A long-legged grasshopper appears to be,
> That springing flies, and flying springs,
> And in the grass the same old ditty sings.
> Would he still lay among the grass he grows in! (Bayard Taylor, trans.)

Unfortunately, the German poet continues, man – like the grasshopper – finds himself again grounded in dirt and muck.

The source for the growth of the inner self is *Affirmation*, what is called by the Arabic word *Eemaan* in Islam. Only by the act of affirmation does all that is external become connected with the internal, with what is vital and real. This is the most important psychological act. Affirmation is never by argument. Only understanding brings affirmation. There is little wonder that the most valuable asset a man possesses is his understanding. The deeper he understands, the higher the level he occupies in the scale of conscious life.

Negation, which is known by the Arabic word *Kuf'r* in Islam, is the Mephistophelian denial of all that confers on life its noblest values and imparts abundance, richness and plenitude to it. Denial always leads to an inner deprivation, to loss of meaning, to superficialities, and—in the end—to perdition. To deny is easy, to affirm is hard indeed. When a man sets out on the path of negation with ill-will in his heart, he can find, wherever he may turn, the proof and corroboration he looks for to justify his denial and rejection. In his own eyes, he appears to be a defender of all the conventional but false values and beliefs of his tribe. The power of negation is terrible and on the surface triumphant. Everywhere there are destructive legions behind it, and nothing would appear to withstand its onslaught. A life of negation is a life of spiritual blindness, of merely superficial existence. It shuts out man from all evolution to a higher, conscious life.

Man blindly gropes his way in a dark world, using a limited form of understanding that can never give him the answers to the most important questions that vex his spirit. The destructive power of *negation* surrounds him on all sides. Affirmation arises only in the real "I," that is, in the true sense of self. This is *to be*. Negation can never erase it. All its satanic power is impotent in the face of this assertion, the "yea," we might phrase it, which creates all the finest values of life.

Every activity, whether a man thinks or feels or acts, uses psychic energy. Yet energy belonging to the state of "consciousness" is of a different order entirely. Mere thinking or mere feeling cannot bring about consciousness. A man, having reached a certain stage of insight and understanding, can create conditions in his inner self to "produce" consciousness. When ordinary thinking, feeling, desire, and sensations are suspended and his inner self is in profound stillness, there is a surge of a state, which can only be described as *consciousness*, and his whole self is filled with a kind of light, through which he is enabled to *see* the nature of things as they are, without veils, illusions, and deceptions. What consciousness is and how it wells forth in the inner self of man is a mystery—a mystery which language is at a loss to describe. Very complex processes can take place without consciousness, or almost in its absence. The "mind" of the Moving Center, for example, makes very complex movements in skating, or in playing a technically difficult piece on the piano, such as a sonata by Beethoven, without consciousness. All sorts of intelligent metabolic processes continually go on in the human body without consciousness. Consciousness is not memory. This gift of God is therefore a marvelous acquisition in man, and it is this *consciousness* whose highest form, known as "Cosmic Consciousness," takes man to the heart of the inner nature of things. A man who has reached Cosmic Consciousness is on the highest ladder of life, still a creature of God, but sovereign and master of all the eye of his *heart sees and reveals.*

There are three degrees of consciousness: the first is consciousness of one's own self; the second consciousness of others; and the third consciousness of Reality. It is this last which is Cosmic Consciousness.

This light, described as *Al-Nur* in Sufi terminology, or "consciousness," is the inmost, indefinable essence of our spirit, least separated from the Divine. An expansion of consciousness means not only that a man that a man sees in the clearest light what has been obscured or hidden from him, but also all the opposites, contradictions and paradoxes, interacting and resolving themselves in harmonious processes, the parts in relation to the whole and the whole in relation to the parts, all finally dissolve into the Cosmic Whole.

To "awaken" is to become more and more conscious by letting in light or consciousness into the dark places within. Consciousness, it should be starkly clear, can never be shared with another person. Each individual stands on his own, most ever to remain remote in the fine sense of this experience. Consciousness would be much too dangerous for them in the somnambulistic state in which they pass their existence. They would lose their sanity and identity.

To become a worthy receptacle for this grace of God, a man should strive to make his life as rich and universal as possible, and with all his "getting" attain understanding. Understanding is the pivot and axis of higher life.

We are carried in the stream of life in a state of "unawareness." We scarcely feel our own existence and the existence of others is far too remote for our notice and consideration. The people who move and walk in the streets and bazaars are "strangers" to our unfeeling selves. They make no impact on us. They do not touch our lives, and we show complete unconcern and indifference to them as persons. There is a woeful lack of understanding among human beings. If other lives touch us, they do so in a negative manner. Our eye is disapprovingly critical. We feed on mistrust and misunderstandings. No man is brother to another in this state of "unawareness." Hate, suspicion, jealousy and resentment poison our lives. How is it ever possible in this miasmic condition to feel vividly our own existence or the existence of others, who dwell in the "outer darkness," so to speak?

A conscious man is based on affirmation. He does not negate or deny. There is no jealousy, envy, hatred, malice or violence in him of which to catch hold. He is deep in his heart and broad in the reach of his mind, and these qualities enable him to understand what comes within his ken and to bear what has to be endured silently and patiently. His own desire is to understand others and to help them understand themselves. He sees himself in others, for they are a mirror to his own self. He cares neither for praise nor blame. He overlooks the shortcomings of others as he realizes that they know no better. In fact, he carefully overlooks their faults and failings and suppresses any fact that would produce discord.

In a state of "objective consciousness" or "Cosmic Consciousness," a man would know the true nature of things. He would pass from the world of appearances to a vision of Reality of inconceivable import and meaning. Mystic and prophetic consciousness is of this stamp and quality. Mystic consciousness reaches "unitary experience," but it does not want to return to the world of flesh and matter. Prophetic consciousness is therefore revolutionary and earth-shaking in its results and consequences, for it comes back to the world to re-shape and remold it in the light of profound insights it has brought back with it. In a few veiled and mysterious verses, the Holy Qur'an describes two mystic experiences of the Prophet Muhammad (peace be upon him), reproduced here in a by necessity inadequate translation:

> By the star when it setteth, your compatriot
> erreth not,
> Nor strayeth he from the way,
> Neither speaketh he from impulse.

> The Qur'an is no other than the revelation
> revealed to him:
> One strong in power taught him, endowed
> with wisdom.
> With even balance stood he
> In the highest part of the horizon:
> Then descendeth he and draweth near,
> And was the distance of two bows or even
> closer-
> And he revealed to the servant of God
> what he revealed:
> His heart falsified not what, he saw:
> What! Will ye dispute with him as to what
> he saw?
>
> - Holy Qur'an (53: 8-12)

No one can describe a higher state of consciousness to another who has not himself experienced it. This is because it is an experience unique in its essence and quality, and it would remain most personal and could never be passed on to another person, even though there may be affinity between the two.

In those awesome moments, which would have shattered any man who did not stand at the highest level of being, the Prophet received the profoundest revelation of the ultimate nature of Reality ever vouchsafed to a mortal by God. In this way, mystic consciousness may just lead to quietism, and no one can describe a higher state of consciousness to another who has not himself experienced it. This is because it is an experience unique in its essence and quality, and it would remain most personal and could never be passed on to another person, even though there may be affinity between the two.

A highly evolved man may appear deceptively simple, and if one passed him by in the street, he would appear no different from others. However, he (the Holy Prophet Muhammad, peace be upon him) is one of the exclusive few, scattered over the earth, the elect of God, attending to His Divine decrees in a veil of secrecy. The scales of God have to be kept balanced, lest man's iniquities upset them. Men go about their task ever so quietly in their respective spheres, and—although the world appears no whit better than before—they fulfill their missions, and this celestial globe moves on to its predestined goal. The devil and the sage play their roles in the manner assigned to them, and the world continues to sweep majestically through outer space, round the sun, in the constellation.

It would not be possible for an ordinary man to live among persons who have attained cosmic consciousness, for the distance between them would be astronomical. Böhme described an experience of cosmic consciousness in these words: "I can only liken it to a resurrection from the dead." Indeed, the state of the "sensual mind" for him was like death. Another experience gave him the feeling that he was gazing into the very heart of things. He saw "the essence and use of properties" and he "knew the being of all things" in that supremely conscious state.

Our senses are veils which hide the nature of Reality from us. What of man then? There is the lucidity of consciousness, the gleam that comes from the light of God. Yet God is beyond the range of man's vision, however inspired it may be. He exists, as a mere mortal, in the shadows, and the "light" is beyond the beyond, open to cosmic consciousness alone. In that experience, there lies a felicity, a bliss, which has the taste of Paradise (*Firdous*).

A man's level of consciousness and his level of being are closely intertwined. We mortals are assigned a destined "space," and for us all things are weighed and measured carefully by the Lord, as King Belshazzar learned to his regret: "Thou art weighed in the balances, and art found wanting." (Daniel 5:27)

The journey to higher levels of conscious experience is most arduous and dangerous. Yet at the same time, it is much too strange and wonderful for mere words to express. This journey has to be embarked upon alone, all by oneself. There is utter silence; there is no living creature one can encounter. There are dark shadows of the night, dreadful places, abysses, treacherous landslides, dreadful storms, icy winds alternating with sizzling heat – taken altogether, it is a most risky undertaking. The perils are daunting, and yet the traveler may delude himself into believing he possesses powers which are not yet his. Long before he has reached the end of the journey, he may claim to have already charted the whole course and call himself the true guide of the unknown way.

Shaik Ahmed Sarhandi, a great Sufi, belonging to the Naqshbandi Order, calls the higher levels of conscious experience as "Stations" of the *Qalb* (the heart). A man has to pass through many "stations" before he reaches cosmic consciousness. He enumerates the stations such as *Ruh, Sirri-Kafhi*, and *Sirri-Akhfa*. He elaborates on each of these "stations," which together constitute what is called "Alam-e-Amr" (the world of Directive Energy). Each has

173

its own characteristic states and experiences. After having passed through these "stations," the seeker of "light" gradually receives the illumination of the "Divine Names" and "Divine Attributes" and finally the illumination of the "Divine Essence." Such observations have not escaped the pens of poets:

> Art thou in the stage of "life," "death," or "death-in-life?"
> Invoke the aid of three witnesses to verify the "Stations."
> The first witness is thine own consciousness-
> See thyself, then, with thine own light.
> The second witness is the consciousness of another ego-
> See thyself, then, with the light of an ego other than thee.
> The third witness is God's consciousness-
> See thyself, then, with God's light.
>
> - Sir Muhammad Iqbal, *The Reconstruction of Religious Thought in Islam*

> "O Thou who art veiled in the shrouds of Thy
> Glory, so that no eye can perceive Thee!
> OThou who shinest forth in the perfection of
> Thy Splendour, so that the hearts (of the Sufis)

> have realized Thy Majesty! How shalt
> Thou be
> hidden, seeing that Thou wast ever
> manifest; or
> how shalt Thou be absent, seeing that
> Thou art
> ever Present, and watchest over us?"
>
> - Ibn Ata'illah as-Sakandari of
> Alexandria (Egypt), *Al-Hikam al-Ata'iya*

The one word that has cosmic dimensions is "Grace." Without God's grace, no person, no matter how very keen and ardent he is, will ever be able to climb the stages and stations to the final height of Cosmic Consciousness. He must first transform his ordinary self, indeed transcend himself, in order that he may become a worthy receptacle of His Grace. For what, after all, is man without the Grace of God? As Hesse reminds us in the "Stages" poem within *The Glass Bead Game*, the Universal or Cosmic Spirit does not seek to confine or limit us but to "broaden us" with each stage.

CHAPTER 19

Metanoia and Meaning

"Die before you die."
- Prophet Muhammad, Holy Qur'an (53: 8-12)

"We become by ceasing to be what we are."
- Sir Muhammad Iqbal, *The Reconstruction of Religious Thought in Islam*

Christ said: "Except a corn of wheat fall into the ground and die, it abideth alone: but if it die, it bringeth forth much fruit." (John 12: 24) To "die," a man must free himself from a thousand petty attachments to things of the world and to "awaken" fully to himself, however painful the process is. To "awaken" means to realize one's limitations, one's mechanical nature, one's negativity, and in the deeper sense one's helplessness, all in clear, simple and concrete facts—*in one's own facts.*

When a man begins to know himself, he discovers that he has within himself many things which are undesirable. He comes to realize that he has nothing which he can truly call his own. This awareness of his shortcomings and limitations will eventually give him the courage to "die" and to renounce forever those aspects of his character which impede him in his inner growth.

If an acorn lies and rots on the ground, it is eaten by a pig; yet if it germinates and grows into a tree, it has another destiny. After all, without "dying" in the chrysalis, the caterpillar could not become a butterfly.

Man is not born as a mechanical being, but he becomes mechanical without ever being aware of it, so deadly are the effects of habits and daily routine on him. His work, his play, his talk, his thinking, his praying, his movements— each and every one of them takes on the character of the "mechanical," and his life loses all the spontaneity, freshness and vitality that it would possess if it did not get reduced to the "mechanical." Everywhere, in most circumstances of ordinary, day-to-day life, man has allowed himself, quite unknowingly, to slide into mechanical ways, and he remains blissfully unconscious of this pervasive fact until his death. His mechanical attitude has far-reaching results on all facets of his life, and there is nothing that he does, things, or feels that escapes the consequences of it.

A man who does not speak from his own understanding is dumb, because he cannot say anything real. A man who does not see the meaning of things is blind. He has eyes, but he cannot see the nature of things, events and situations. Further, a man who does not hear anything with his inner ear is deaf. Most of us are deaf, dumb and blind, oblivious of the nature of reality.

> They have hearts wherewith they understand not, eyes wherewith they see not and ears wherewith they hear not.
> - Holy Qur'an (70: 179)

Having eyes, see ye not? and having ears,
hear ye not? and do ye not remember?

                                    - Mark (8: 18)

For the LORD hath poured out upon you
the spirit of deep sleep, and hath closed
your eyes: the prophets and your rulers,
the seers hath he covered.

                                    - Isaiah (29: 10)

The mechanical behavior of others sets irritation in us, though our own behavior is mechanical too. The so-called *good* too are mechanical in their goodness, and if we were living among them, we would be just as irritated as we are with others. They would give us a feeling that they were "asleep," not really being aware of what they were doing. How unreal even a "good" life can be!

People find the "bad" interesting and exciting, and they hold the "good" insipid and dull. All negative manifestations of life have a strange pull and power and they have an impelling force, which appears deceptively "free" from the mechanical effects of habit and routine. Real "goodness" is rarely seen and felt, and its impress is healing and binding and uplifting, for it is completely free from all traces of mechanicalness. Much of the so-called "good" seem dull and uninteresting, while the "bad" shine for their cunning and cleverness. The ordinary "good" and "bad" are the attributes of somnambulistic man. The difference is one of degree. The so-called "good" can quietly and easily pass into the "bad." There is no absolute "Bad" or "Evil." There is, however, an absolute "Good," and any real manifestation of goodness is a part of this "Good." Absolute "Good" belongs to God alone.

All truth is relative to our capacity to understand it. We have to have the perception to see the truth of the truth, so that it can have the right effect on us. Just to hear a truth means nothing. Like all other things, this hearing, too, is mechanical. To hear it with our inner ear, which is understanding with the heart, is quite another matter. How much stands in between!

No compulsion can make a man evolve in and from himself. It is really a question of his own inner choice, a matter of his deepest and most individual understanding. If people were forced to be good and virtuous, and if God loomed threatening in the sky and they were cowed down, then their spirit would be violated and made sterile. They would, as a consequence, do nothing from themselves, from their own understanding and will. How could man evolve under coercion? The human situation would be far worse than before.

The senses do not give us a clear proof, an unmistakable affirmation of intelligence and meaning behind the scheme of things.

Nature is infinitely varied. It is beautiful, yet repulsive. It is prolific, yet unfeeling and unconcerned. It is rank in growth, yet austere and stark. It is awe-inspiring, yet dreadful and menacing. Nature has a thousand faces and moods. Pain and suffering are the inescapable shadows of life. Fear, grief and insecurity haunt man all the days of his life and even make his sleep restless. Corruption and decay claim all things in the end. The wheel of fortune turns, and man comes to sweet or bitter days as her caprice governs:

[The] man [who] hopeth high up to ascend
On fortune's wheel, and come to state
royal
If the wheel turn, may doubt [...] to
descend —
If he be high, the [worse] is his fall.
            - Sebastian Brandt, *The Ship of Fools*
                (Alexander Barclay, trans.; revised
                            slightly by editor)

As the world presents aspects inimical and alien or monumentally stupid and absurd, man goes through his earthly existence unable to fathom it all. It is impossible to judge or decide anything if we start from life or nature, and this in itself is an extraordinary, mind-boggling situation. *Life proves nothing.* There is the apparent cruelty of nature, creature feeding on creature in a ruthless war for survival against coldly indifferent laws regulating the whole phenomenal world.

Confronted with this situation and arguing from the state of the visible world, is it possible to believe that God exists? This problem is the first to engage any earnest and thoughtful person. The result is doubt and pessimism, more often than not. Is not the atheist who bases his conclusion on the cruelties and tragedies he sees in the world right, in his own way, to judge that life does not seem to show the existence of God?

A thought or emotion cannot be seen or touched, nor a dream a man dreams in his sleep. Yet they are as "real," as these whirling energy-entities and their effect on life is so inclusive and pervasive, especially of "thought" and "emotion," that life cannot be conceived without them. How perverse is man's approach to the fundamental problems of the "how, why and whither" of these Cosmic questions. If we searched in the material world for the evidence of the existence or non-existence of God, nothing would come of it. Questioning life anxiously and being influenced by what happens in the world, with all its accidents, injustices and miseries, is to miss the meaning of the Teaching of the Prophets. No one, whoever he may be, can change the laws that govern this Earth. Anything can happen in life, for "time and chance happeneth to [...] all" (Ecclesiastes 9: 11). It is senseless to get upset and dismayed when we hear about the most tragic and frightful things that occur anywhere in the world.

Ironically, the Universe created by God would not be perfect if it did not also include "imperfections." Perfection necessarily implies completeness. It must include everything, just as a complete color-chart not only contains the beautiful and pleasing colors but also the whole spectrum from the "whites" to the dull, dirty, depressing grays, browns and blacks, in all their differing shades.

The key-board of the piano covers the full scale of notes, from major to minor, from flat to sharp. It is only in a succession of these notes, varying in pitch and tone, that music is born. The harsh keys are just as necessary as the soft to create harmony.

God's decree is in its totality, irrespective of whether we regard it as good or bad. It is not the evil aspect of the manifestation that He decrees, but the manifestation as a whole, which is an inevitable expression of His Law. The contradiction, in so far as it could contain what would appear to us as "evil," exists only for man, who is ignorant of the decree behind all God's manifestations.

How could the Universe we live in exist if there were good and no evil, light and no shadow, joy and no sorrow, beauty and no ugliness? Binaries are ineluctable in the very scheme of things. Else we would be living in quite a different Universe, with other laws than those that operate in ours. Where there is pain, grief, sorrow and suffering, there is grace, mercy, joy and love, all woven together in the tapestry of life.

The Holy Qur'an says:

> We offered the trust unto the heavens and
> the earth and the mountains,
> But they shrank from bearing it and were
> afraid of it. And man assumed
> it. Lo! he hath proved a tyrant and a fool.
> - Holy Qur'an (34: 72)

This trust man had "assumed" was moral freedom, which "the heavens, the earth and the mountains" did not possess. He alone had taken upon himself the burden of a free, moral agent, with fateful consequences.

Man could never avoid or shrink from this painful, very irksome responsibility thereafter. Even not to act is an act of choice. In this constant challenge and response man has to live his life and make or mar it. Were he coerced to do, without his own free choice, then his "doing" would not be moral and he could not be held responsible and accountable. For perception to be "perception," it—by definition—has to be one's own.

Man would be a mere robot had he not been given free will, within the limits imposed by the laws of life, the order of things, to exercise his choice between "good" and "evil," "right" and wrong," for it is by test and trial alone that man could evolve and work out his own destiny.

As man develops in knowledge, insight and understanding, his conception of what is evil and what is not evil undergoes a change: of what has to be truly sought and what has to be resisted. He then discovers that "good" and "evil" are not two absolutes, opposing each other. There are really two "goods," one relative, the opposite of "evil," and this is *mayavic* (alteration of state or "becoming"). The other is an absolute "good," and this is an attribute of God, in so far as human understanding can conceive Him, for attributes are neither He nor not He.

If there are forces of evil and darkness, of chaos and confusion, this viewpoint is entirely man's; it is his very human but limited way of looking at things, of surveying reality.

It is his quality and level of consciousness which enable one man to see "evil" where another sees both "evil" and "good" in an indivisible relationship. Evil is the inevitable consequence of man's freedom of choice, necessary so that he may grow and evolve. At times it hinders him, throwing him into an extreme imbalance, into a false relationship with objects, events and situations, causing estrangement from God. It tests him in a thousand devious and subtle ways, throwing road-blocks in his path of self-evolution.

"Good" is that which ennobles and elevates him and sets him towards higher conscious life, turning him away from ill-will, craving, ignorance and unreality to the direction of light, freedom, unity and wholeness.

"Evil" is the distortion and falsification of Reality. It regresses man to depravity, dark guilt and fragmentation. It drags him down to what is low, base and mean and makes him a slave of passing impulse that possesses him. Everything evil touches turns into blight. It makes man perverse, obdurate and contumacious in all his ways.

At the heart of things there remains the paradox that "evil" ultimately serves the ends and purposes of "good."

Goethe, in his profound insight, understood this. When Faust asks Mephistopheles the Devil who he is, the reply of that cold, mocking spirit of denial and rejection is

> Part of that Power, not understood,
> Which always wills the Bad, and always
> works the Good.
>> - *Faust, Part I* (Bayard Taylor, trans.)

This is the cosmic meaning of "evil." Satan is the Companion whom God has given to act as a gadfly, for this Temptor drives man through temptations to ever new trials and tribulations. It is in man's nature to "err." Man passes from guilt to remorse and from remorse to more guilt. He falls, rises, falls again, and rises again. He gropes and strives – all of this just as Goethe (in the portion of *Faust* quoted earlier) describes man as a grasshopper, striving to fly and yet falling back into the muck in an ever-continuous cycle. These rises and falls, from the "grays" of his acts to the glimmers of light, proceed until death comes to snatch him away from his last gropings and puts an end to his strivings as well as misadventures. Until then, man's energy longs for rest and repose that he may eat lotus, like the lotus-eating inhabitants Odysseus saw when he visited "the land of Lotus and the flowery coast" of Homer's imagination.

When man rises to a higher state of conscious life, he discerns lucidly that there is really only relative "good," ever in conflict with relative "evil," that there is no absolute evil, only an absolute good at the heart of creation. Yet our perspectives are much too narrow for us to relate them to larger and higher meanings of the Cosmos. This truth was observed by Alexander Pope in epigrammatic form in his *Essay on Man*:

> All nature is but art, unknown to thee;
> All chance, direction, which thou canst not see,
> All discord, harmony not understood,
> All partial evil, universal good...
>
> *- Essay on Man*, Epistle I

How easy it is to lose our sense of balance, if we possess it, when troubles and cares press us down and we find life hard to live and bear. In ordinary life, who has sufficient detachment to weigh his own troubles and difficulties in balance with others? Man, in his egoism, feels smug and complacent when his personal situation works to his own advantage. Yet the moment it affects him adversely, he whines and wraps himself up in self-pity.

Being self-centered and indeed selfish, man would never want to move away from ease, comfort and sensual pleasures. Pain and grief, when they do come, and must come, far from leaving him chastened, only make him embittered. He blames his fate—even blaspheming God— for his misfortunes. Little does he realize that his own excesses and inadequacies are the cause of his troubles and pitiful state. It is not something that a "wrathful" God has unjustly visited upon him. He has to emerge from his own ignorance of himself and of the fundamental order of things that governs his and all organic life. The laws of life are the very expression of the Will of God, and human life receives its worth and meaning only when man lives his life in conformity with them. He then is in tune with the spiritual order of things and is no longer under the tyranny of his impulses. All negative states, especially lying, pretense, duplicity, hypocrisy, avarice, jealousy, envy, hate, ill-will and sloth flout the laws of life. Not to conform to them is to destroy both the body and the spirit.

When man *cares* to conform his life to the fundamental order of things, his life emerges from darkness into light, from unreality to reality, from slavery to freedom. He has come to *understand* the nature of things. He now understands his own self, and in understanding his own self, he comes to understand others. He has come to learn the right attitude towards everything. This creates a right and enlightened relationship in his dealings with the world.

Only a fully integrated man, upright and clear-sighted, can attain this level.

Others, without being aware of the nature and consequence of the network of relationships, live for themselves and only for themselves, sunk in their petty and selfish interests and desires. Theirs is a life of "denial" and "rejection," opposed to the will of God. Hubris, the Greek term for "excessive pride," possesses them. It is the last state of blindness and obduracy and is also known in Greek as *ate*. This is when man is most remote from God, and it is then that evil appears attractive and most desirable. Man persistently distorts and falsifies reality, and all his ways turn iniquitous:

> Those whom God sendeth astray (they
> who flout the fundamental
> order of things and live a life of denial and
> rejection) there is no guide
> for them. He leaveth them to wander
> blindly on in their contumacy.
>
> - Holy Qur'an (7: 186)

CHAPTER 20

God, Time and Consciousness

We cannot understand anything rightly unless we realize the nature of "Time," which is both real and unreal as we know and feel it. Man cannot define time, nor can he explain it, for it is unique in its nature and essence, utterly unlike anything known to him. The life of the spirit is in "time" far more than it is "space." Thoughts and feelings have no spatial dimensions. They have only temporal succession, a "before" and an "after."

For all organic beings, "time" means life itself; all must respond compulsively to the passage of time. The alternation of day and night, of summer, winter, spring and autumn, of the equinox and the solstice, the phases of the moon, of its cycles of waxing and waning — one and all have a lasting effect on human and animal behavior and on organic life in its biological processes. There is an innate sense of cyclical time in all living organisms. They are orientated to a twenty-four hour period. This metabolic beat is called the "circadian" rhythm. Any tampering with or disturbance of this rhythm has a vital bearing on the physiological and psychological well-being of all living things.

Yet it appears there is no absolute reality to time. Indeed, what "time" is on earth is not what "time" may be in other worlds in the Cosmos far out in the limitlessness of outer space. Were man to travel through the awesome depths of the Universe, his conception and "feel" of "Time" would be so strange and "out of the world" that the "earthlings" could never conceive of or imagine it.

Man is earth-bound, and all Outer Space is really above and beyond his ken. It is too hostile and even hazardous for him to survive so far out of his element, as he is constituted. The extent to which he undertakes journeys into Outer Space can only be under very special conditions and controls. It would never be possible for him to experience the actual physical environment of the worlds in the Cosmos, for he must be encapsulated in specially designed space suits, and this would mean that he would take with him the earth atmosphere he is used to and live and breathe in it. How is it then ever possible for him to experience what "Time" is, its nature, essence and taste, in Outer Space? He will be left to make artificial "constructs" and nothing more. The "reality" of "Time" out there will forever elude him.

Our ordinary level of consciousness is intimately related to our idea of "time," whereas higher levels of consciousness experience the transcendence of linear time, for psychic time is very different from linear time.

Even in the usual sense, no two persons may have the same perception of time, and this perception changes in one and the same man, according to his mood and condition. "Time" is relative to his state. How strange that the "taste" of "Time" changes with changes in his psychic and psychological states! There is a world of meaning hidden in this "fluid" time. It is here where the seeds for the experience of Cosmic Consciousness lie.

A second of intense agony may seem excruciatingly long, an "eternity" to one man, while a blissful state lasting for some length of time may appear to flit by like a brief moment to another.

Many qualities of "time" streak through our ordinary waking state of awareness. As we have seen in Ecclesiastes, there is a time for joy and a time for grief; there is a time for play and rest and a time for work and labor (3: 1-8).

In a dream, a man may live through many years while in fact only a few seconds may have elapsed. In hypnosis or under anesthesia, one may enter a state of consciousness in which a few moments may seem to last months and even years.

The quality of "time" varies from day to day, and it is magically different at dawn and at noon, in the evening and at dusk, and during the four watches of the night. There is a period in the deep of night when man, in a state of consciousness, may experience himself enveloped in a pure, chaste, holy "time." which may properly be regarded as a beam of eternity and in these moments he "feels" the presence of higher beings ascending to and descending from "heaven" and the Earth as if washed clean of sin and guilt. As the Metaphysical poet Henry Vaughan wrote of this perception at night:

> I saw Eternity the other night,
> Like a great ring of pure and endless light,
> All calm, as it was bright;
> And round beneath it, Time in hours, days, years,
> Driv'n by the spheres
> Like a vast shadow mov'd...

Time has such subtle nuances that if man were to live his life fully attuned to its marvelous rhythms he could never feel bored and jaded. Every moment would be lived intensely.

Time is different in the various Centers in man and each Center, again, has its own "time." Thus, "time" has a different quality and taste in each Center. How strange and wonderful that is!

Time is doubtless a dimension of all living beings, whoever they are, and inner time is the very fabric of a man's life.

Much of the fear and anxiety from which man suffers is an expression of time. When he is in conflict with time, fear and anxiety take hold of him. Stress and strain sap him when he tries to make time run faster or when he clings to the past and vainly attempts to ward off the uncertainties that haunt his future.

The value of passing time would appear to fluctuate as a man goes back into his past or leaps into the future.

A man's life is his time. He may share the same things and the same interests with others, but he is in his own time as others are in theirs. This points to the unique individuality of man. However, when his life is imprisoned in mechanical habit and routine, time is no longer an integral element of his being.

Although a man's body is of one age, he is all ages internally.

A man's portraits at different periods of his life are images in three dimensions of a being who is actually a four-dimensional creature, and he continues to retain his identity all through the flux of the organic, chemical and psychological processes that make up his life from birth to death. He changes from moment to moment, and yet he remains the same being.

In linear time, infancy appears very short and old age very long, but in physiological time, this is reversed, and infancy appears very long and old age very short. Paradoxical as it may seem, "aging." is rapid in the beginning of life and slow in the final period of maturity. Yet a year is much longer for a child than it is for a man, and as we age, we realize the truth expressed by Hafez:

> The span of thy life is as five little days,
> Brief hours and swift in this halting-place;
> Rest softly, ah rest! while the Shadow delays,
> For Time's self is nought...
> (*Divan*; Getrude Lowthian Bell, trans.)

Yet it is important to remember that chronological age is not the same as physiological age. True age is physiological and is measured by the rhythm of the changes in the organic and functional states. Individuals vary in their rhythms. Some remain young well past middle age, while others grow old long before their time. Their organs wear out early in life.

We live among people of every age, those whose "time" lies ahead of them and those whose "time" lies behind them, and they all meet in the "present" moment. We have consequently the strange fact of different "times" meeting in the same "time." and the same "space" contains different temporal worlds of the young, the middle-aged and the old.

"Time" changes at every interval we move. There are different rates of the flow of "time." The faster we move, the slower becomes the flow of time for us.

Time and interest are connected. When a man says he has no time, as often as not, he means to say he has no interest. If one is interested in something, one will – somehow – find time for it.

We "gain" time or we "lose" time. We "save" time or we waste" time. How short is a second and how long is an hour? Inconceivable things can happen within the duration of a second, and millions of years are mere "seconds" in the age of the Universe.

No one has ever seen a "place" except at a certain "time" or felt a "moment" except at a certain "place." "Time," then, is a space interval in our recognition of an "event." There is therefore no difference between absence in "time" and absence in "space." Man could never be conscious of an empty, eventless time, and there could be no event without time.

A "year" is the name we give to the measure of the progress of the earth in its elliptical orbit around the sun. A "being" living on the planet Mercury would witness an orbit around the sun in just eighty-eight of our earthly days, and in the same period it would rotate only once on its axis. Therefore, a year goes by at a much more rapid place when seen from the planet Mercury, and thus time passes quickly or slowly according to one's vantage point or perspective — "one planet after another closes one eye for a longer or shorter time," as Novalis poetically phrases this relative nature of time in the galaxy. (Frederic H. Hedge, trans.)

Yet "Time" is ultimately something so much deeper. Though "time" in itself is confused with man's awareness of time, it has the most profound cosmic significance of its own.

The sidereal heavens "float" majestically at awesome speeds in "astronomic time." The atom, on the other end of the scale, whirls in "electronic time," which is the measure of radioactive movements within the atom. The living organism exists in "biological time." They, all of them, have their own "time-scales," and there is no correspondence whatsoever between these, nor can there be one.

There are many different currents of "time" on the cosmic levels and planes and within the dimensions of the Universe. These currents originate in the central "ground" of Eternity and finally return there. This is something very difficult to grasp, for how can man's feeble and very limited understanding reach those regions of Cosmic operations, forever hidden in enigmas?

It is said that beyond the speed of light "time" comes to a stop. It is true as far as the human mind can comprehend it.

With "instantaneity," only "pure Duration" remains. This may be described as Now, an eternal, living "moment" that stays forever.

In man's "I," which is a universe in itself, there are many measures of "time," again, most fittingly, with a central core of eternity. The real "I" of man, in its most luminous state, resides in that core, where there is no foothold, no height, no depth, no length, no breadth—an awesome Silence, impossible for the mind of man to grasp.

Man is confined within time and space of this Earth, and yet his thought and consciousness can soar far beyond the limits imposed upon his physical self. The whole Universe is within the ambience of his mind and consciousness. Clairvoyance and telepathy are expressions of the power latent in him.

"Time" and "change" are inseparable. They are the twin masters of our world, whose very soul is irreversible movement and perpetual flux is its permanent condition.

There are tendencies in things that vary from time to time, and similar things tend to happen together under the Law of Synchronicity.

Time is invisible. No object has only three dimensions; it has also the dimension of "time," or it would just vanish.

We see the Universe in the past, as it was. We do not see where the stars are at the present moment, but where they were in the past. Their "past" is our "present." It would indeed be very awkward if the same thing happened to the objects around us. We would see them, but we could not touch them.

If we could halt at one moment of "time," everything would remain exactly as it was positioned. Nothing would move.

The World exists not only in the "present moment." It is there in the very dimension of "Time" itself. There is a World in "Time," in a space of more dimensions than our mind can ever comprehend. We can touch these higher dimensions at a point which is defined as Now.

In the most luminous state of consciousness, man discovers himself in the inner "timeless" still center in the ground of his being. He finds himself in the eternal

Now and realizes the truth of Sri Krishna Prem's words: "He who sits within the heart is throned beyond all Time."

The Prophets of God had the power of vision to see into events lying far ahead of their time. They had two "sights" – the one which an ordinary man has and the other which penetrated the higher dimensions of Time.

God transcends both Time and Space. He is no more in Time than He is in Space. To God, *all is at once*, instantaneous, not successive. All is "present," and we are existent just at one point of this limitless "present." Mekander of the Shaiva Siddhdantha concludes that "To God, there is no time. All things are to Him one consentaneous whole."

It is to this Eternal Present that the word "remaineth" refers in the Qur'anic verse:

> All that is therein (in the created Universe)
> suffereth extinction and
> there *remaineth* the Countenance of thy
> Lord in its Majesty and Beauty.
> - Holy Qur'an (55: 26, 27)

This Eternal Here embraces and enfolds "before" all beginnings and "after" all ends.

The Qur'an touches on the nature of time in the following verses:

> And put thy trust in Him that liveth and
> dieth not. Celebrate His praise
> Who in six periods created the Heavens
> and the earth and what is between them,

> then mounted His throne; the God of
> Mercy.
>
> - Holy Qur'an (25: 58)

Time has a different meaning or reality in far-out space, and perhaps the *"six" periods* allude to a conception of Time, in a Dimension, beyond the earthly comprehension man. In the words of the Qur'an, one Divine Day is equal to 50,000 years:

> The messenger -spirits and the (great)
> Spirit ascend towards Him daring a Day
> the measure of which is 50,000 years.
>
> (70: 4)

The feeble mind of man would find it difficult to grasp the nature of this notion of Time. The process of creation lasting through ages and eons of Time, as understood by man, is expressed as a single, indivisible act of God, Take this verse from the Holy Qur'an:

> All things We have created with a fixed
> destiny. Our command was but one, *swift*
> *as the twinkling of an eye.*
> (54: 49-50; emphasis that of the author)

How is it ever possible for man to apprehend the meaning of this Time? Man, after all, is "imprisoned" in "serial-time," and all his experience is based on his sensory impressions.

"Destiny" has been described by the poet and philosopher Sir Muhammed Iqbal:

[O]ur conscious experience, is not a string of separate, reversible instants; it is an organic whole in which the past is not left behind, but is moving along with, and operating in, the present and the future is given to it not as lying before, yet to be traversed; it is given only in the sense that it is present in its nature as an open possibility. It is Time regarded as an organic whole that the Qur'an describes as *Taqdir* or the destiny [...] Destiny is time regarded as prior to the disclosure of its possibilities. It is time freed from causal sequence - the diagrammatic character which the logical understanding imposes on it. In one word, it is *time as self* and not as thought and calculated. [...] Time regarded as destiny forms the very essence of things. As the Qur'an says: "God created all things and assigned to each its destiny." (25:2)

The destiny of a thing is not an unrelenting fate working from without like a task-master; it is the *inward reach* of a thing, its realizable possibilities which lie within the depths of its nature and serially actualize themselves without any feeling of external compulsion. Thus, the organic wholeness of duration does not mean that full-fledged events are lying, as it were, in the womb of Reality, and drop one by

> one like the grains of sand from the hour-
> glass. [...] To exist in real time is not to be
> bound by the fetters of serial-time, but to
> create it from moment to moment and to
> be absolutely free and original in creation.
> In fact, all creative activity is free activity.
> Creation is opposed to repetition, which
> is a characteristic of mechanical action.
> (*The Reconstruction of Religious Thought
> in Islam;* italics by the editor)

The Qur'anic verse "Every day doth some new work engage Him" (55-29) touches on God's uniquely free and original creative activity, transcendent and absolutely beyond the comprehension of man's intellect. It implies a Universe that is intensely dynamic, and a continuous process of new and fresh creation never stops. There is nothing static about this Universe. Time, from whatever plane or level it is viewed, is also dynamic, in keeping with the dynamic nature of the Universe.

God's "time" is the "Eternal Present." This is Eternity, in which there is no past or future, only a "present." Meister Eckhart, the great German medieval mystic, says cryptically: "If I take a portion of time, it is either yesterday or today. But if I take now it will include all time." ("Detachment" treatise; Sister Odilia Funke, trans.) Little wonder that William James, in discussing Meister Eckhart, notes "the paradoxical expressions that so abound in mystical writings." ("Mysticism," Lectures 16 and 17, *The Varieties of Religious Experience*)

To a different being, the serial-time of man might appear a duration in which he may be experiencing another kind of change quite unlike ours. Our own experience of passing-time makes nature appear to us what she is. What she is to herself, however, is quite another matter. Processes that take millennia may be merely "moments" on her scale.

If we were to reverse "time," we would witness a radical change in our own life and in the meaning of events and situations. We would see graves open up and the dead stand and walk out of them alive. Bullets which had been shot from rifles would shoot back into the barrels. The jacket a man has taken off his back and thrown onto a chair would rise from there of its own accord and fly on to his back. If a man tried to shoot another, the bullet would refuse to hit and kill him. All violence would at once cease. No object could be lost. "Backward" time would give rise to another causality. It would be an utterly novel world and it would defy all the notions we have of "up" and "down," "movement," "far" and "near," fast" and "slow" and a thousand other things that obey our law of causality.

It would be like Ezekiel's vision of the valley of bones:

> ... there was a noise, and behold a shaking, and the bones came together, bone to his bone... lo, the sinews and the flesh came up upon them......and they lived, and stood up upon their feet... (Ezekiel 37: 7-8; 10)

We live in three-dimensional world, and this gives rise to a perception of objects which is only relatively real. The present moment is an infinitesimal part of Reality, extended in dimensions beyond our understanding and existing in directions of which we can have no idea. Add a dimension, and you are presented with entirely new relationships.

The German mystic Böhme says man "falls asleep in time." In point of fact, he falls "asleep" not only in "time," but also in "matter" and in himself. He is a "sleep-walker" who somehow survives his walk on the ledge of a wall and dies from other causes. He is never *really aware* of what is happening to him. If he ever *wakes up*, he *wakes up* too late. At that moment, he is beyond the grave, on the other side of death. Yet as Hildegard of Bingen, another German mystic, enjoins us that the "heart can waken" first from its "age-old sleep" and experience the spiritual reality around us in the present.

Our experience of passing time profoundly affects our thoughts and feelings. We seem to live the most fragile of existences in an ever-perishing world, fugitive creatures living precariously in a fugitive world. There is nothing stable or permanent, nothing secure; all is evanescence. We hang by inches on a cliff, below which there yawns a bottomless abyss.

The ancient Hermetic literature enjoined the seeker to expand himself "to the magnitude of all existence" if he desired to reach a higher level of understanding and consciousness.

The "present moment" of a man's life is a point in the *magnitude* of his existence. All moments of his life can be considered as "present," stretched out in consciousness throughout its entire length. All the incidents, events and situations can be re-experienced, re-lived in an actual sense, hard to express. It is not just memory. *All is.* Nothing is lost. In moments of imminent death, for instance, all the events, situations and incidents of the whole past are etched out in very sharp mental images which evoke most vividly forgotten scenes to the mind's eye. The French poet Baudelaire, in one of his poems ("Le Parfum"), speaks of an incense which "restores the past."

All things and all possibilities are in the womb of Eternity, which is not a prolonged infinity. It is without "duration" and without "successiveness." It is a Now that cannot be described in any language. This Now stays fresh and unchanging. Behind Eternity there is God, and behind phenomenal reality there is Eternity, which could be called, in a sense, a "thought" of God, developed in all its fullness in all the "dimensions" of the Cosmos. "Time," as we know and experience it, may be said to be a "moving image," a "trace of Eternity," made manifest to our puny understanding. It is just an expression of this "Whole."

The distinction between "time" and "Eternity" is qualitative and psychological. Eternity is "structured" in Unity. Time is built in "number," as our experience of it shows us.

Ecclesiastes says all things are "subject to time" in our World and men are creatures *of time.* Yet God "hath set eternity into their heart." (3: 11, American Standard Version) Man has therefore been set apart from all other created things.

If we were to understand the meaning of this, then psychologically "eternity" is the "full" state of being in man. "For thus the world will possess an imitation of the perpetuity of eternity; not having only the half, but the whole of the infinity of time," in the words of Proclus (Thomas Taylor, trans.). Man then "abides in one" in unity and wholeness.

This idea of "wholeness" and its meaning in its relationship to "eternity" has been given beautiful expression by Boethius, a Roman senator and Neo-Platonist of the fifth century, who wrote his famous and eloquent book *Consolation of Philosophy* in prison while facing a death sentence for treason:

> [E]ternity is the possession of endless life whole and perfect at a single moment. What this is becomes clearer and more manifest from a comparison with things temporal. For whatever lives in time is a present proceeding from the past to the future, and there is nothing set in time which can embrace the space of its life together. It grasps not yet tomorrow's state, while it has already lost yesterday's; even in the life of today, one live's no longer than one brief transitory moment. [...] Accordingly, that which includes and possesses the whole fulness of unending life at once, from which nothing future is absent, from which nothing past has escaped, this is rightly called eternal; this must necessarily be ever present [...] and hold the infinity of movable time in an abiding present. [...] Plato ascribed to the world that it is one thing for existence to be endlessly prolonged, another for the

whole of an endless life to be embraced in the present, which is manifestly a property peculiar to the Divine mind. God need not appear earlier in mere duration of time to things created, but only prior to the unique simplicity of His nature. [...] for the Divine anticipates all that is coming. He transforms and reduces it to the form of his own present knwoledge and varies not, ever attaining, but in a single flash forestalls and includes mutations without altering. This ever-present comprehension and survey of all things God has received comes not from the issue of future events but from the simplicity of his own nature.

(H.R. James, trans.; passage edited by Lisa Berberian)

The "future" never *is*, for the moment it registers as the "present," it becomes the "past." This process is inexorable in its character. Man can do nothing about it. His life is circumscribed by this fleeting moment, to which he ascribes, in his illusion, the "present." There never really is a "present." Man cannot keep his own state of being more than a moment, for as soon as it arises, it vanishes in the past. His experience is one of continual loss, for the successive moments, which constitute *his states of being, never staying with him.* They appear only to disappear *at once.*

We see only a point of time and then another and so on in a series we call "present moments." We only register what we call the "present moment," not the "past" or the "future," which has no real existence for us. All possible existence we limit to this doubtful thing called the "present moment." Yet the paradox here is we are never in contact with or conscious of this "present moment," as it is so small and fleeting. It is actual and yet it is doubtful—not to the senses, but to our consciousness. The "present moment" is a mere line with no magnitude.

Our consciousness is a confused thing, composed as it is of the "past," the "present" and the "future." We live in the past or in the future, behind or in front of the "present moment." We can never find ourselves in it, for we always live elsewhere in our thoughts, fantasies and imagination, either in the past or in the future. Our "past" or our "future" are merely parts of our "elsewhere." As strange as it may appear, we are, as it were, not present in the external world psychologically. Now *real life* is in the "present moment," not in memories or regrets "of the past, nor in hopes or fears of the future." Each "present moment" is eternal, for it is both in time and in eternity. Eternity suffuses every "present moment" in passing time, for he who succeeds in living in the "present moment" truly lives, lives authentically. This is the reason why we experience "eternity" in a higher conscious state, and why certain things from the past stand out so vividly.

Man exists then both in time and in eternity.

Eternity is *vertical* to serial-time, and the direction of higher levels of conscious experience is vertical: the intense awareness of oneself Now. Every "Now" is eternal.

It is with eternity that we must connect all latent possibilities. To be fully conscious is to possess the feeling of "Now" – "I" distinct from the past or the future, and thus the "newness" of oneself, the "I" Now. In that supreme state of consciousness, one becomes aware that "eternity" is always in the Now.

Therefore the authentic "I" is in eternity, not in serial-time. Most fittingly, therefore, behind this authentic "I" is God.

In our ordinary state we traverse passing-time, seeking to complete ourselves and make no attempt to give any dimension to our lives. We see and feel nothing of the marvelous coherence and unity of the Cosmos. We see only multiplicity on all sides without any clear relationship or meaning. Now halts passing-time, which is displaced. Now is a living and luminous state. In that state a man *IS*, free from all earthly encumbrances. The highest understanding, deepest insights and intuitions, and "revelatory" senses repose in Now, bathed in "divine" light. We withdraw into the holiest and the purest sanctuary within us, which is the focal point of the ground of our being.

Our authentic life lies in the higher dimensions, which are realities of our interior life. The most radiant and lucid feeling of "I" lies behind the multiplicity of our conditioned personality, that which is engrossed in the world, with all its stress and strain of ambitions, impulses, negativity and fears, and anxieties. Inherent in this state of "light" is Now.

As Sir Muhammad Iqbal writes in *The Reconstruction of Religious Thought in Islam*:

> Existence in spacialized time is spurious existence. [...] It is only in the moments of

> profound meditation, when the efficient
> self is in abeyance, that we sink into our
> deeper self and reach the inner centre of
> experience. [...] It appears that the time of
> the appreciative-self [the inner self] is a
> single "now" [...]

This is sempiternal existence.

We *see* the nature of Reality in Now. It is here we reach the center of things.

What distinguishes the "quick" and the "dead?" It is this luminescent state on which the Now focuses.

Consciousness of the Now may result by a man's self-control and a divine-grace "elevation," as Meister Eckhart phrases it, of "the natural faculties to union in God above the merely temporal objects of existence." ("Outward and Inward Morality" sermon, Claud Field, trans.) Albert Pike, writing some sixteen centuries later, posits a similar thought: "Among the primary ideas of consciousness, that are inseparable from it, the atoms of self-consciousness, we find the idea of God."(*Morals and Dogma*, Chapter 28)

A man is then *present* to himself in the very core of his being. He resides in Now, the consciousness of which leads him to the Divine.

Can we understand Holy Qur'an at all unless we realize that the recurring theme, treated in chaste, austere, majestic and lyrical language, is the higher states of conscious experience?

The creation of the world begins in man himself. At first, all is darkness, then light appears and is separated from darkness, the light of inner perception and understanding, which begins to dissolve the ambient gloom.

The man who is unawakened can be compared to "a ship, sailing in the sea, [which] leaves no traces of her way behind her" (to borrow words from the third-century Christian theologian Hippolytus; S.D.F. Salmond, trans.). This is man in serial-time.

The right response is the only answer to Cosmic challenges to man. The Universe itself is an infinite response. To everything that is authentic in us, the universe gives in "good measure... and running over" (Luke 6:38), and because response in its plenitude spills over, the evil force of "Negation" as a Cosmic counter-force leads man, in his state of obduracy and contumacy, to the lowest depths he can sink. When we give up trying to understand, we not only stop but even begin to disintegrate. The "ignorant" are really those who cling tenaciously to what hinders them.

Are we not in two "places" at once—one in the outside world and the other in the interior world of self? If we were to realize this in all its depth, we would know that what we do Now is the only important thing in life. In the presence of higher meanings, all debased meanings that so fill our lives in serial-time shrink and shrivel up, and we are redeemed from all that is petty, trivial and base.

CHAPTER 21

The Liberation of Man

Everything in the Universe, from constellations to man and from man to the atom, either evolves or devolves, rises or descends, develops or runs down. Even in Roman Antiquity, the poet Lucretius (who knew of the atom long before modern science) observed the truth that "time changes the nature of the entire universe, and one condition of things after another must succeed in all things: nor does anything abide like itself. All things move and change." (*On the Nature of Things*, Book V, 828-830; W.H. Mallock, trans.)

Nothing in the Universe can be static, but nothing can ever evolve "mechanically." Only decay and devolution happen mechanically. That which cannot evolve consciously only degenerates and disintegrates.

The only form of evolution which is destined for man is "conscious evolution."

Man has seven categories, to use the language of conscious evolution.

The first three categories embrace what can only be described as the "ordinary man."

First there is the "Physical Man." In him, the Moving Center is most active. This Center is the magnet of his psychic life. The "physical man" spends most of his life in games and sports, acrobatics, dancing, racing, acting, climbing, and the like. He lives in physical movements and sensations and generally *cares little* for things of the mind or of the spirit.

Second comes the "Emotional Man." Emotions govern him. He revolves around the "Emotional Center" in him. He is always moved and swayed by feelings and sentiments. The heart is far more important for him than his mind. Most of his decisions, in whatever the situation in life, are influenced by and based upon his feelings and sentiments.

Third is the "Intellectual Man." All his emphasis is on reason. He argues and theorizes but distrusts the heart and the magnet of his life is his Intellectual Center. The scholar, the theoretician, the mathematician, the philosopher and the bookworm represent this category. Most often the man who emphasizes the "head" and belittles the "heart" has a desiccated life. Pure intelligence without the fusion of conscience is dangerous. Lucifer, the Prince of "Intellectuals," is its fitting symbol. This form delights in futile discussions, arguments, destructive criticism in an intricate exercise of equivocation, which medieval scholasticism well illustrates.

Every man is born within these three categories. One man is distinguished from the other by the "Center" that is most active in him.

Fourth is the "Balanced Man." The "ordinary man" evolves into the "balanced man" by efforts of a definite character. He makes use of all his psychic centers properly, being fully aware of the importance and uses of all his centers and calls on their different meanings, shades and nuances. He tries to see objects, situations and events from different angles and sides and arrives at an opinion or a decision after weighing the various aspects he has observed. He does not judge harshly from one narrow, rigid attitude of "right" and "wrong" or "good" and "bad." nor does he put others in a "prison." As a result, his view is broad and spacious. Active tolerance is a habit of his life. This does not come from any weakness or indifference. Its source is rather inner calm and strength. He is aware of many things in his being, which were dark to him before and for which he was apt to blame others. He does not waste his time complaining and finding fault with others. He is conscious of the full swing of the pendulum, so that neither one side nor the other has any grip on him. The tensions of the opposites are dissolving into harmony. He is moving away from the subjective elements in his knowledge to *objective* knowledge. He is becoming objective to himself, clearly showing the inward reach to the center of his being, which is free from all polarity and contraries. To sum up, he is "awake." His mind's eye *sees*. His heart *understands*.

Fifth is what may be called the "Unitary Man of the First Stage." He has intimations of higher conscious states. His knowledge is *whole* and has an indivisible "I," the indispensable quality of an evolved man. What he knows the whole of him knows. This is a very significant fact about him. His knowledge is far more objective than that of the "balanced man."

Sixth is the "Unitary Man of the High Conscious Stage" with new knowledge and new powers, such as the power of controlled telepathy. He has attained higher levels of conscious experience. His knowledge, however, can still be lost, as some of the things he has acquired have not yet become permanent. The "Sage," wherever he may be found, East or West, is the best example of the Sixth Category. He stands close to the "Complete Man."

<u>Seventh</u> and last is the "Complete Man." He has attained full objective knowledge, consciousness and will. He has evolved to the apex of life and no man could go further. Everything in him is his own and whatever is his can never be lost. It truly belongs to him. He stands on the highest level of being, as he is the most highly evolved man on earth. In Arabic he is called Insan-ul-Kamil, which means "Complete Man." He is, in the spiritual sense, master of his own destiny. He lives wholly in tune and harmony with the permanent order of things, what may also be called the Laws of the Cosmos. It is through him that the essential unity of the Universal and the particular is fully realized. He can pass without any transition from his unique knowledge and consciousness of the nature of Reality to action in the world of man, from the vast sweep of cosmic ideas to the smallest details of life. The highest example of the "Complete Man" is the Prophet Muhammad, peace be upon him. He was in every sense of that expression "Insan-ul-Kamil." No other man in history could ever reach the height he reached.

The *understanding* of Insan-ul-Kamil is the highest understanding man can ever reach. All "understandings" are only different approximations of or degrees to this "understanding."

At the ordinary level, there are as many understandings as there are men. Each one understands things in his own particular way. Yet then we should call this "understanding" wholly subjective. A man approaches a situation or an event in life in accordance the degree of understanding he has come to possess in his commerce with the world.

A "being" created perfect has made no effort of its own to its growth and development. Man, by descent and ascent, is superior to the angels, who have been created "perfect." Abstract purity or absence of temptation, conflict, urges and desires can be no test of virtue or perfection. What is imperative is the possibility of choice, which makes man unique in all of nature, for he alone possesses the freedom of choice.

Man's spiritual development should not be at the expense of the other *sides* of his nature. His physical urges are an integral part of his nature and are not the consequence of an "Original Sin," which is the bedrock of Christian faith. The evil disposition is not original in his essence, for nothing except pure negation can issue from original evil. Man is born with a being, or nature, which is urntainted and innocent, free from guilt, untarnished, according to the Teaching of Islam. Man affirms and he denies. These are both expressions of his moral freedom. If depravity were inherent in his nature, the choice between good and evil would just be illusory. In order that he attains full *selfhood*, the imperative demands of his body and the aspirations of his spirit have to be so integrated that all the facets of his indivisible nature come to express themselves fully in balance, proportion and harmony.

This is the "Unitary View of Life," which is the quintessence of Islam.

The study of man, Nature and the Cosmos, which influence one another so profoundly at every moment of time, must never be pursued piecemeal. Nothing happens anywhere in the Universe without leaving its trace on all other things therein. All meanings are in "relationships." Time, space, causality, entities, events, one and all, finally dissolve into a single process, in which everything is part of all else. All meanings lie entirely in the relationship of the parts to the whole, and the whole to the parts.

The one worthy aim and object of man is his liberation from the bondage of things. He realizes this intensely when he "awakens" to his real situation on this earth. This is really the most basic thing for him to undertake, for the stark fact is he somehow becomes a *slave* within and without in his pursuit of worldly goals.

To cast off "slavery," a man must go through a very painful process of shedding off his ignorance of himself and of the nature of the world he inhabits. Without self-knowledge, insight and understanding of the real nature of things, it is not possible for a man to liberate himself. He will continue to dwell in darkness and be a plaything of the forces which are continually acting and reacting on him in the world of appearances. He will never know the reality of things and remain unaware of the meaning and purpose of his life.

When he becomes *free*, he lives, true to himself and true to others, in a creative encounter with reality, the state of "light" when the veils of ignorance, self-delusions and self-deceptions are drawn away from his *mind's eye*, or, more appropriately, his *heart's eye*. He becomes dynamic, yet *still* as a top as it spins its fastest. He steps aside and places himself at an *inner distance* from all things, even from himself. He is in the world yet *not* of the world. (John 17: 16) He is free from caprice, and his life becomes authentic. He is now an "entelechy." wholly committed, wholly responsible, ever alert to capture the essence of things. He comes to possess full human dignity, nobility and universality.

Man is endowed with very great potentialities. At each moment, however, he has to make his choice, and the choice he makes, ironically, limits him. He can rise or fall, or he can stay where he is rooted and stagnate. He makes his own choice and decides, within the limits imposed by the order of things under which he has to pass his existence: his own fate.

Nothing can be attained in an unawakened state, for an unexamined life is a life passed in slavery. In the consciousness of a wayward, egocentric man, his self-deceptions, illusions and fantasies are mixed with reality. He lives in a small, mean part of himself, shut in and self-divided, transfixed in one spot. This is "death" in life. The poet Coleridge posited this thought, though in different verbiage, when he wrote "The Night-Mare LIFE-IN-DEATH [...] thicks man's blood with cold" in *The Rime of the Ancient Mariner*, a work keenly aware of the need to expand man's horizons and nature beyond appearances and the visible.

Man's nature has an infinite range. Whatever has been given to him as a human-being can take him to the peak of self-evolution or drag him down to Cimmerian depths, the "lonely land, and gloomy cells" in Homer's *Odyssey,* where

> endless night invades,
> Clouds the dull air, and wraps them in
> shades. (Book XI; Alexander Pope, trans.)

215

All rests on his choice, on the manner in which he makes use of his faculties. Everything is right in its proper place, and even pain and grief have their uses. They are a part of his existence, as are all polar opposites. How else is he to become human and spiritual in his aspirations?

Yet man's hubris knows no bounds, even though he is pathetically haunted by the specters of fear and anxiety, impermanence and insecurity, and mystery wraps the whole of creation. He worships all manner of idols, be they power, money, possessions, status or obsessive feelings for objects. He makes himself slave to his impulses and is buffeted here and there and blown in all directions. He sets no proper value to human dignity, remaining supremely unconcerned as to how to become truly human. Balance, harmony and wholeness he will not seek. His life takes wrong turns throughout its course.

What, then, is the sum of his life?

It remains tragically inadequate, perversely squandered, and very far indeed from all the brilliant promise that was instinct in man's seed. Man becomes a sad caricature of the godlike being he was created to be.

The whole of life is learning how to die to oneself in order how to live.

To know how to die is to know how to live.

CHAPTER 22

Conclusion

This study on the states of man—man's psychology, intellect and spirituality from an all-encompassing, universal perspective—concludes with a survey of the vast canvas we have traversed. It is a study which has taken us through astronomy, metaphysics, philosophy, and—of course—faith, very often through some of the greatest books ever written in the history of mankind.

How appearance differs from the reality of things is an insight many writers, philosophers and religions have noted about the nature of the world and our experience of it. This dichotomy between appearance and reality is reflected in how our individual being is a divided self, living simultaneously in a world of illusion as well as objective reality. The five senses can actually hinder man from getting into touch with his trace "self." In a sense, human destiny is a search to realize the inner self, developing character and an ability to fulfill and shape one's own destiny. In an effort to achieve this, man would do well to have an awareness of the psyche and its various centers.

A distinction, however, must be made between essence and personality. There is a distinction between knowledge and being, but when harmonized, they create understanding. Understanding others is needed for empathy, yet many do not even have an understanding of themselves. Even people who think about themselves constantly do not have the observation or awareness to know themselves well, for arrogance and condescension against everyone else—towards others—often get in the way.

Human beings have an extraordinary ability to imitate others, but this ability and the aforementioned arrogance make it difficult for human beings to construct a unique persona and develop positive attitudes towards the world. For most, a persona is just a collection of random attitudes we take on by osmosis or from our largely negative emotions. Emotions here are defined as constant but momentary reactions to states determined by feelings which are set attitudes, pride, violence and mendacity as well as other "vices" descend from such emotional states for the person who has not developed a sense of self and equilibrium.

Most men, in effect, live in a world of illusion largely determined by the emotional states. One such illusion is that of words, which have their origin in emotion. Yet words are not arbitrary, but have a mystical association with things. Still, words can create a barrier, as we often observe when we attempt to formulate our most solemn ideas in speech or writing. The communication of prayer is therefore more effective in expressing the state of inner awareness.

A modern and yet ancient problem of man is boredom. Boredom is psychological entropy, for if we are aware to life and its multi-faceted possibilities, we can scarcely be bored. Boredom is really, at base, a fraudulent suffering. Though memory can also cause real suffering, it is a gift which allows us to relive the most pleasurable experiences and reinvent them as we strive towards a high level of consciousness.

Causes and means matter greatly in the development of our growth and our realization of increased consciousness. More than merely providing a moral compass, causes and means help us to understand the nature of the universe and reality. Nature is a duality of opposites, and religions and cultures around the world have gleaned this insight from reality. Man himself swings back and forth on a pendulum of extremes. It then takes self-knowledge to put this in perspective and achieve inner balance and thus break free from the life most men lead of narrow-minded prejudice, complacency and – as Thoreau might say – of "quiet desperation."

The nature of the universe is one of paradox. On the one hand, base instincts are a constant in human nature. One the other hand, on a cosmic level, the universe is of a nature which is well proportioned as the planets move regarding their various orbits and revolutions.

Philosophers, sages and prophets have come to teach human beings to strive for a sublime understanding of the world and God. In a sense, different prophets arrive to teach one and the same truth, varying only in form to suit the special conditions of each community. Literary artists play a crucial role in bringing about realizations on the essence of life, for God makes use of parable, symbol, allegory and related rhetorical strategies. The awe-inducing power of God is contrasted to the true Nature of the Will, for the Will of the emotional center of man is the essence of life.

Man approaches knowledge of God and self-awareness through mystical insights which bring about consciousness in a synthesis of perception, insight, intuition and understanding – a drawing together of feelings and emotions into a harmony. Having greater awareness necessitates an embarking on a journey towards the interior life beyond the veil of illusions and self-deceptions. Growth of the inner self requires Affirmation, what is called *Eemaan* in Arabic.

There are three degrees of consciousness: consciousness of self, of others and of reality. Most men are caught up in everyday mundane affairs of life and thus live in a state of unawareness. To adapt a verse of the poet Sir Muhammed Iqbal, consciousness is life and the state of unawareness and the state of unconsciousness is "death-in-life."

Another duality is that of good and evil – good being defined as that which ennobles and elevates man towards the higher, conscious life and evil that which debases man to depravity and fragmentation. Paradoxically, "evil" in its cosmic sense ultimately serves good, for whatever "wills the Bad [...] always works the Good." (Goethe, *Faust*) Blasphemy, blaming God for the existence of evil and even denying the existence of deity, are small-minded reactions to the inadequacies of man and one's own misfortunes.

Time is at once real but also relative. Our experience of time varies as we survey the past and our own memory. When we leave the bounds of earth and contemplate outer space and the universe, time becomes a dimension and exists on so many planes that the human being cannot even hope to fathom. If Time and Space from the cosmic perspective become unfathomable to contemplate, so much more so is this true of God, for he transcends both Time and Space. God's "time" is the "Eternal Present," and this we call Eternity. As the German mystic Böhme noted, man "falls asleep in time" and is unable to truly grasp Eternity. Man's consciousness is a confused thing, composed as it is of the "past," the "present" and the "future." Man lives in the past or in the future, behind or in front of the "present moment." To be awakened to Life itself, we must strive towards an understanding of time which contemplates eternity.

Man's liberation – his "breaking free from a state of self-induced immaturity," as Immanuel Kant says in the context of his essay "What is Enlightenment?" – requires transcendence from his physical and emotional states to intellectual and balanced stages of developments and then finally to a development to a unitary and then complete nature. Then man shall become truly conscious and know how to live and how to die in harmony with the universe.

In this study, we have contemplated many of the grand philosophical issues which have confronted mankind for millennia: the meaning of life, the problems of suffering and death, man's search for God, transcendental self-awareness, and a greater understanding of the mysteries of life. At the same time, this study has proceeded in humility with full knowledge that it does not and cannot claim to be a discussion which puts any of these issues completely to rest. This effort should be viewed rather as an attempt to bring attention to these essential branches of human knowledge and a plea to the reader to strive continually for a contemplative life, for this is what matters in the end (*Faust*, Part II, line 11936). Those who seek ultimate answers to all the meanings of life may find, with Blaise Pascal, "They do not know that it is the chase, and not the quarry, which they seek." *(Pensées, No. 139).* There are perhaps no better words to end this study than those of the nineteenth-century American philosopher Albert Pike, who provides us if not with the final words on these topics then with a clear direction and guide as he writes that "the noblest purpose of life and the highest duty of a man are to strive incessantly and vigorously to win the mastery of everything, of that which in him is spiritual and divine, over that which is material and sensual; so that in him also, as in the Universe which God governs, Harmony and Beauty may be the result of a just equilibrium." (*Morals and Dogma*, Chapter 32).

A Treasury of Great Books: Books Quoted or Referenced

"Writers may be classified as meteors, planets and fixed stars. [...] They belong not to one system, one nation only, but to the universe. And just because they are so very far away, it is usually many years before their light is visible to the inhabitants of this earth."

—Arthur Schopenhauer, "On Reputation" (T. Bailey Saunders, trans.)

"There is nothing that so greatly recreates the mind as the works of [...] classic writers. Directly one has been taken up, even if it is only for half-an-hour, one feels as quickly refreshed, relieved, purified, elevated, and strengthened as if one had refreshed oneself at a mountain stream."

— Arthur Schopenhauer, "On Books and Reading" (Mrs. Rudolf Dirks, trans.)

Perfect understanding of a classic work should never be possible; but those who are cultivated and who are still striving after further culture, must always desire to learn more from it.

—Friedrich Schlegel, *Lyceum and the Athenæum* (Louis H. Gray, trans.)

N.B.: The list of Great Books referenced and discussed is indexed chronologically. Numbers refer to chapters, not pages. "F" refers to the Front or Title Page, "P" refers to Preface, "R" to "Remembrance," and "T" to the "Treasury of Great Books" Index. For subdivisions of the Holy Bible, biblical books are ordered according to their sequence in the Holy Bible. All quotes from the Holy Bible, including the Deuterocanon (Apocrypha), are from the King James Version ("Authorised Version") of 1611, unless otherwise noted. Translations from the Holy Qur'an are authentic and recognized.

Classical and Biblical Antiquity

Middle Ages, Islamic Golden Age, and Sufism

Renaissance and Baroque

Enlightenment

Nineteenth Century

Twentieth Century to Present

Okakura Kakuzō, *The Book of Tea*, **R**
D.H. Lawrence, *Phoenix*, **18**
Joshua Loth Liebmann, *Peace of Mind*, **9**
Lin Yutang, *The Importance of Living*, **P**
H.L. Mencken, *The Antichrist* (trans.), **14**
    A Mencken Chrestomathy, **P**
W.H. Mallock, *Lucretius on Life and Death, in the Metre*
    of Omar Khayyam (trans.), **18**
George Orwell, *Nineteen Eighty-Four*, **10**
Sayyadana Osman, *Silent Sermon*, **18**
Sri Krishna Prem, **20**
Elaine Pagels, *The Gnostic Gospels*, **14**
Ayn Rand, *Anthem*, **2**
Milton Steinberg, *Basic Judaism*, **14**
    "A Mystical Note," **14**

Printed in the United States
By Bookmasters